AXEL, by VILLIERS de l'ISL...

Philippe-Auguste, Comte de Villiers de l'Isle-A... Brieuc, Britanny, in 1838. He came of an ancie... eccentric family, fervently Catholic and steeped in chivalric tradition. He lived mostly in Paris, making literature the sole object of a vagabond existence, and suffered atrocious poverty until his death in 1889. His writing has a powerful poetic quality, concealing a mystical philosophy beneath an ornate and extravagantly decadent romantic style.

Axel is the epitome of symbolist drama, and gave its name to the definitive work on decadence and symbolism, Edmund Wilson's *Axel's Castle*. "Count Villiers de l'Isle-Adam," wrote W. B. Yeats, "swept together words behind which glimmered a spiritual and passionate mood, as the flame glimmers behind the dusky blue and red glass in an Eastern lamp." Villiers started Axel at about the time he became acquainted with Wagner, in 1869, and worked on it during nearly two decades. Over this period his own metaphysical enthusiasms moved from occultism, through more orthodox idealisms and back to Catholicism, which he had never ceased to practice. Each of these positions is examined in turn by Axel, Count of Auersperg and by Sara, an escaped nun of heartbreaking beauty whom he discovers in the vaults of his storm-swept castle. Each is rejected and it is with the dramatic discovery of the highest ideal, amidst tumbling cascades of gold and jewels, that the work ends.

VILLIERS DE L'ISLE – ADAM

AXËL

TRANSLATED BY M.GADDIS ROSE

A SYMBOLIST DRAMA

PUBLISHED BY THE SOHO BOOK COMPANY
1 BREWER STREET LONDON W1

MCMLXXXVI

Published by
THE SOHO BOOK COMPANY
1/3 Brewer Street, London W1R 3FN
1986
First published as a book in French in 1890
First published in this translation in 1970

British Library Cataloguing in Publication Data

Villiers de l'Isle-Adam, Auguste
  Axel.
  I. Title II. Rose, Marilyn Gaddis
  843′.8[F]   PQ2476.V4

  ISBN 0–948166–05–3

Printed and bound in Great Britain
by Redwood Burn Ltd, Trowbridge, Wiltshire

INTRODUCTORY NOTE

The life of Jean-Marie-Mathias-Philippe-Auguste, Comte de Villiers de l'Isle-Adam was as cruel and poetic as his work. "An exceptional tale," says Mallarme, "at the extremity of which is the tomb." He was born in Saint-Brieuc on the Northern Coast of Brittany in 1838. His grandfather had been ruined during the emigration and his father completed the destruction of the Villiers fortune by buying estates at inflated prices in order to excavate them in search of buried treasure. Villiers himself, in his application in person to Napoleon III for the vacant throne of Greece, betrayed a hereditary eccentricity. He left Normandy for Paris at seventeen, and devoted his life to literary enterprise which he saw as the only glory of the age. His *Premieres Poesies* were published in 1859. He was haunted by Baudelaire, whom he met in a cafe and whose Satanism seems to have disturbed Villiers' religious instincts. It was Baudelaire who released him from the outdated Romanticism of his earlier years. In 1862 he published the first volume of *Isis*, a philosophical romance. By the mid 1860s he was a prominent member of the Parnassians and a close friend of Mallarme. He was seen as the most promising man of letters of his generation. Nine days he spent with Wagner in 1869 provided an inspiration that was second only to Baudelaire's, and it was while revisiting Wagner during the Franco-Prussian war in 1870 that he met Nietzsche. He started *Axel* between these two visits, following Wagner's advice about turning to an ideal world, and continued to work on it over the next 20 years.

Like *Faust*, with which it has often been compared, *Axel* is a philosophical drama written to be read rather than performed. It contains the whole essence of symbolism, it is symbolism deliberately taken too far. It is a "drama," wrote W.B. Yeats in his introduction to the play, "which is written in prose as elevated as poetry, and in which all the characters are symbols, and all the events allegories."

With the death in 1871 of the rich aunt who had supported him, Villiers' resources came to an end and he entered a period of poverty and darkness. Literary frustrations, lawsuits and the failure of political and publishing schemes blackened the 1870s and early 1880s, but during this period he continued his work on *Axel*, "attempting to embody in a stage action a conception of a transcendental kind". This period also saw the ripening of his friendship with Huysmans (Villiers is one of the Duc des Esseintes' favourite writers) and a return of some degree of literary success balanced by growing ill health. The *Contes Cruels*, his most widely read book, came out in 1883. *Axel* was published in sections during 1885; deepening fears of damnation led him to attempt to alter the moral content of the play at the last minute, by changing a few words in the closing scene just before it went to the press.

During 1885 and 1886 the word Symbolism came into fashion to designate the group of young writers led my Mallarme, Verlaine and Villiers. He was suddenly famous. Maeterlinck, who came to know him at this time, said of meetings with Villiers that "we had the impression of being the officiants or the accomplices of some piously sacriligeous ceremony, on the other side of the sky." A subscription by friends kept him from starvation, but continuing financial problems had a worsening influence on his health. "Villiers de l'Isle-Adam", says Mallarme, "wrote the last pages of *L'Eve Future* lying flat on his stomach on the floor of a room emptied of its furniture and lit by the stump of a candle." As his condition deteriorated, a growing Christian belief led Villiers to attempt again to suppress the anti-Christian pessimism of Axel, which he came to regard as his spiritual testament. Perhaps fortunately for the play, he did not have time. Stomach cancer was diagnosed in May 1889 and the realisation that he might die before being able to perfect his life's work turned him against God; from his hospital bed he was known to be planning a lawsuit between God and himself. He married on the 14th August 1889 to legitimise his son and ensure the continuance of his line and on the 18th said to his wife 'Hold me tight, that I may go gently' and died. Huysmans and Mallarme, his literary executors, corrected the proofs of *Axel* which was finally published in 1890. In a lecture given after his death, Mallarme called him: "The man who never was, save in his dreams."

CONTENTS

To My Parents

TRANSLATOR'S FOREWORD

A year after seeing *Axel* February 26th, 1894, one of the two performances at the Théâtre de la Gaîté in Paris, Yeats wrote, " Count Villiers de l'Isle-Adam swept together . . . words behind which glimmered a spiritual and passionate mood, as the flame glimmers behind the dusky blue and red glass in an Eastern lamp; and created persons from whom has fallen all even of personal characteristic except a thirst for that hour when all things shall pass away like a cloud, and a pride like that of the Magi following their star over many mountains ". Yeats never claimed to know more than the rudiments of French. He admits in his preface to H. P. R. Finberg's translation in 1925 that he read *Axel* originally " as learned men read newly-discovered Babylonian cylinders ". So it is safe to assume that he could follow only the mood and movement of the five-hour performance (billed as a " récitation ", although it used sets, costumes, and an orchestra and chorus for Alexandre Georges' music). It was a mood of sombre yet erotic exaltation, a movement of solemn yet heterodox liturgy, all bound to be congenial at that time to the writer of *The Countess Cathleen*. Over a quarter century later when he wrote " Stories of Michael Robartes and His Friends " as a disarming introduction to *A Vision*, his estimation had changed, and he could use *Axel* as material for a joke. In this introduction he presents an amoral girl who calls herself Denise de l'Isle-Adam and who nonchalantly distorts the characterizations, even attributes a key speech to the wrong character. Yeats, monolingual compared with Pound, Eliot, or Rilke, was probably the most appreciative spectator *Axel* could have had. *Axel*, significant because it is the epitome of Symbolist drama, is, paradoxically, unsuccessful because it is. In expanding every Symbolist tenet, in exploiting every preferred Symbolist image (he seems to have missed only Mallarmé's swans and Rimbaud's alphabet blocks), Villiers made *Axel* more a definition-demonstration than a play and so doing made it in the end perhaps too explicit for Symbolism. In short, we should read it through the red and blue prisms of Yeats's selective impressionability. We should filter out Villiers' amazing fusion of

Symbolist tendencies and leave in shadow the verbiage around it.

Villiers, monolingual himself, was nevertheless deliberately Wagnerian and Poesque. (He became personally acquainted with Wagner in 1869, about the time he started on *Axel*, but he could not read in German those operas which he used to play and sing in drawing rooms. He gave Poe recitations as part of his repertory also.) Although *Axel* could be considered a combining and amplifying of the *Igitur* and *Hérodiade* which his friend Mallarmé never finished or a popularizing of the work of his sometime spiritual guide Eliphas Lévi, it reads also like *Tristan and Isolde*, if the Celtic lovers killed themselves in the ecstasy of Act II,* or " Ligeia ", if Poe gave more attention to the co-operation of sex and will.

During the nearly two decades that Villiers worked over *Axel*, his metaphysical enthusiasms, always hostile to the positivism of his times, moved, roughly, from occultism through more orthodox idealisms back to orthodox Catholicism, which he had never ceased to practice. Hence, although Axel may very well represent Villiers, he speaks through the characters in turn. The symmetry of the play alone makes that clear. Sara, Axel's life-clinging female counterpart, has the last word and the last gesture, and into the mortuary of the dawn *Liebestod* comes the murmur of life, resuming dominance as the curtain falls. Villiers scrupulously negates the attraction of heterodox monasticism in Act I, secular retreat in Act II, occult liberation in Act III, and death-consummated love in Act IV.

Rigorously symmetrical, as typological in structure as the *Oêdipus* cycle, *Axel* is woefully awkward and unbalanced in execution with perhaps the most tedious second act in modern drama. Characters, speeches, props, sound effects—all have counterparts and come into the play like counterpoised operatic leitmotifs, culminating finally in the destined confrontation of the encompassing Female (Eve — Sara — Emmanuèle, the wife-mother bringing grace) and the axial Male (Axel). From separate but

---

* See A. W. Raitt, *Villiers de l'Isle-Adam and le mouvement symboliste* (Paris : José Corti, 1965), p. 137.

similar supernatural disciplines Sara and Axel, each twenty-three years old, distant cousins, come face to face and resist together the ambiguous fascinations of money, wanderlust, and passion.

On Christmas Eve, Act I, Sara, the more aggressive and virile of the two, disrupts her ordination ceremony at a pseudo-Catholic convent in Flanders to begin her search for Axel's treasure. Thus she rejects the cloistral death-in-life promoted by the Abbess, the Archdeacon, and the enamoured novice Aloyse and chooses the life extolled by the carols to the Infant Jesus. With the companionship of a mysterious winter-blooming rose which she lays upon her dagger, secure in the power of the Rosicrucian emblem, she reaches Axel's remote Black Forest castle on Holy Saturday. Here Axel is enduring his own Gethsemane. In Act II he kills his worldly cousin, who extols the claims and opportunities of society. Thus he rejects the death-in-life of pleasure and satiation. (Here Villiers in a misplaced concession to probability lets the movement lapse in endless exposition.) In Act III Axel ignores Master Janus, who extols the claims and opportunities of ultimate reality. Thus he rejects the death-to-life of the esoteric ascetic. He does not notice Sara's arrival in the antechamber, but Master Janus informs us that "The Veil and the Mantle, both renunciators, have intersected: the Work nears fulfilment". In Act IV after deciding upon suicide for himself and immediate betrothal for his enamoured page Ukko, whom he will not abandon as Sara abandoned Aloyse, Axel comes down to the family vault in the early hours of Easter morning. There Sara, after opening the tunnel to the treasure, finds him. Their attempts to kill each other are only the first gestures of the erotic passion to which Axel lets them only verbally succumb. Her sensuous suggestions—all romantic advances are hers—move him so acutely that he will not face their possibly deceptive realization. And she, not from cowardice before disappointment, but from the bravery of feminine self-sacrifice, accedes to his wish. (Like his contemporary misogynist Nietzsche, Villiers shows women more formidable than men.) "Lost in mysterious rapture", she joins him in the only orgasm left to them: death. They believe that they have chosen life-in-death. But is their suicide an exquisite example to mankind? Or a noble miscalculation? Or a sacrifice of superior victims for the continuance of life? Villiers' final stage direction reads, "And—disturbing the silence of the awesome place where two human beings have just freely dedicated their souls to the exile of heaven—are distant murmurs of the wind in the forest vastness, vibrations of the awakening of space, the surge of the plain, the hum of life".

Yeats may have been clairvoyant in the essay quoted earlier when he saw in works of *Axel* not moribundity and decay but quiescent purification. "I see," he wrote, ". . . in the arts of every country those faint lights and faint colours and faint outlines and faint energies which many call 'the decadence', and which I, because I believe that the arts lie dreaming of things to come, prefer to call the autumn of the body". He elliptically indicated not only the message of *Axel* but its place in modern literature: the last glow of the first generation of Symbolists, the last uneasy denigration of the flesh before its restitution in Gide, Yeats, and O'Casey, its relegation to sterility in Proust, O'Neill, and Eliot.

The translator wishes to acknowledge the generous help given by her former colleagues at Stephens College—Professors Cynthia Oehler and Edwin Shepard Miller. She is grateful also to Senator Michael B. Yeats and the Macmillan Co. Ltd. for permission to quote from Yeats's work.

State University of New York at Binghamton, 1968.

xii

Before I went to Paris in 1894 I had read with great difficulty, for I had little French — almost as learned men read newly-discovered Babylonian cylinders — the *Axel* of Villiers de l'Isle-Adam. That play seemed all the more profound, all the more beautiful, because I was never quite certain that I had read a page correctly. I was quite certain, however, that it was about those things that most occupied my thought and the thought of my friends, for we were perpetually thinking and talking about the value of life, and some-times one or other of us — Lionel Johnson perhaps — would say, like Axel, that it had no value. It did not move me because I thought it a great masterpiece, but because it seemed part of a religious rite, the ceremony perhaps of some secret Order wherein my generation had been initiated. Even those strange sentences so much in the manner of my time —'as to living, our servants will do that for us'; 'O to veil you with my hair where you will breathe the spirit of dead roses'— did not seem so important as the symbols: the forest castle, the treasure, the lamp that had burned before Solomon. Now, that I have read it all again in Mr. Finberg's translation and recalled that first impression, I can see how those symbols became a part of me, and for years to come dominated my imagination, and when I point out this fault or that — the monotonous piling-up of pictures in the last scene, the too abundant debates with the Commander or with Janus — I but discover there is no escape, that I am still dominated. Is it only because I opened the book for the first time when I had the vivid senses of youth that I must see that tower room always, and hear always that thunder?

Axel or its theme filled the minds of my Paris friends; my host Macgregor Mathers, magician and mystic, talked of the Rosy Cross, and condemned the Sar Péladan for founding a Rosicrucian Order of his own, and bringing its roses to Notre Dame to be blessed. The Latin Quarter had become virtuous, and notorious young women talked of their virginity. 'Villiers de l'Isle-Adam,' Rémy de Gourmont wrote, 'has opened the doors of the unknown with a crash, and a generation has gone through them to the Infinite.' But when I met Verlaine he insisted, having evidently forgotten all about it, that Villiers meant that nothing mattered but love, and added, 'He was flighty, but what French he wrote!' I met frequently at a friend's house the wealthy Russian woman who had arranged for the play's performance, and I remember her vehemence, her vitality, as she paced to and fro kicking the floor-rugs from her way, and denouncing Ibsen for his lack of morals; and that a young sculptor, who had tried to represent in stone forms like those painted by Gustave Moreau, sat at a little table in the corner modelling a bust of the actor who was to take the principal part. The Sar Péladan had commended portraits that were 'to the spiritual glory of the sitter.' The Russian had in her box upon the night of the performance her three divorced husbands, with whom she remained on the most excellent terms. I was in the midst of one of those artistic movements that have the intensity of religious revivals in Wales and are such a temptation to the artist in his solitude. I have in front of me an article which I wrote at the time, and I find sentence after sentence of revivalist thoughts that leave me a little ashamed. I wrote that we had grown tired 'of the photographing of life' and 'returned to symbolism,' that these realists must be compelled to follow science into the obscurity of the schools, that 'the puppet plays of M. Maeterlinck have been followed by a still more remarkable portent. Thirty thousand francs and enthusiastic actors have been found to produce the *Axel* of his master, Villiers de l'Isle-Adam. On February 26th a crowded audience of artists and men of letters listened, and on the whole with enthusiasm, from two o'clock until ten minutes to seven to this drama, which is written in prose as elevated as poetry, and in which all the characters are symbols, and all the events allegories. It is nothing to the point that the general public have since shown that they will have none of *Axel*, and that the critics have denounced it . . . and called the young generation both morbid and gloomy. One fat old critic, when the Magician of the Rosy Cross began to denounce the life of pleasure and to utter the ancient doctrine of the spirit, turned round with his back to the stage and looked at the pretty girls through his opera-glass. Have

xiv

we not proved, he doubtless thought, that nothing is fit for the stage except the opinions that everybody believes, the feelings that everybody shares, the wit which everybody understands? — and yet they have brought Dr. Ibsen and the intellect on to the boards, and now here comes Villiers de l'Isle-Adam and that still more unwholesome thing the soul.'

I then go on to suggest with a prudence that surprises me that, should the play be brought to England, the second and third acts should be 'enormously reduced in length. The second act especially dragged greatly. The situation is exceedingly dramatic, and with much of the dialogue left out would be very powerful. The third act, though very interesting to anyone familiar with the problems and philosophy it deals with, must inevitably as it stands bore and bewilder the natural man with no sufficient counterbalancing advantage. There was no question of the dramatic power of the other acts; even the hostile critics have admitted this.' And then I wind up by commending the players and producers because they have not forgotten that an actor can be at times 'a reverent reciter of majestic words.'

On my return to London I tried to arrange a performance there, and Miss Florence Farr, who was producing *Arms and the Man* and my *Land of Heart's Desire,* offered her theatre for nothing, but the London public was thought unprepared, being in its first enthusiasm for Jones and Pinero.

September 20th, 1924.   W. B. YEATS

AXEL

DRAMATIS PERSONAE

AXEL, *Count of Auersperg*

THE ARCHDEACON

COMMANDER KASPAR OF AUERSPERG

UKKO, *Axel's page*

HERR ZACHARIAS

GOTTHOLD

HARTWIG

MIKLAUS

THE CELEBRANT OF THE OFFICE OF THE DEAD

EVE SARA EMMANUELE DE MAUPERS

THE ABBESS

SISTER ALOYSE

SISTER LAUDATION, *Nun in attendance at turning-box*

SISTER CALIXTE, *Stewardess*

NUNS OF THE CLOISTER OF ST. APOLLODORA

CHORUS OF OLD MILITARY RETAINERS

CHORUS OF WOODCUTTERS

The action takes place in the last century around 1828 : the first part in the cloister of St. Apollodora, a convent of the Order of the Holy Trinity, situated on the coast of old French Flanders; the three others parts in north eastern Germany, in a very old medieval castle, fortress of the margraves of Auersperg, buried in the depths of the Black Forest.

PART I
THE RELIGIOUS WORLD

Coeurs tendres, approchez: ici l'on aime encore!
Mais l'amour, épuré, s'allume sur l'autel:
Tout ce qu'il a d'humain à ce feu s'évapore,
    Tout ce qui reste est immortel.*

                        Lamartine.

  * Tender hearts, come here to timeless love!
  For chaste love at the altar bursts in flame:
  Dispersed the mortal dross to airs above,
    None but th' immortal essence can remain.

I

And compel *them* to come in !*

The cloister choir of an old abbey chapel.
At the rear, a large stained-glass window. At left, four rows of
stalls.** They rise gradually in a hemicycle against the high circular
grille which is closed and veiled by draperies. At the rear, near
the grille, a low door opens upon stone steps leading to the
cloister.
At right, directly facing the stalls, are the seven steps and parvis
of the high altar, which cannot be seen. The carpet extends into
the centre of the choir to the edge of the tumular flagstone
sepulchres. The golden bell and censers are on the second step.
Baskets of flowers are banked above them. The sanctuary lamp
illuminates only the principal apse between the large supporting
pillars laden with ex-voto offerings ; near one of the pillars a white
marble pulpit dominates the nave and adjoining aisle.
A human form, veiled to its bare, sandalled feet, is standing
beneath the lamp. From the back enter the ABBESS *and* ARCHDEACON
in sacerdotal habits.
The priest kneels before the altar and prays; the ABBESS *comes*
up to the veiled creature and abruptly unveils it.
A face of mysterious beauty appears—a woman's. She is absolutely
immobile, her arms folded, her eyelids lowered. For a few moments
the ABBESS *studies her in silence.*

SCENE 1

[SARA, *the* ABBESS, *the* ARCHDEACON, *then* SISTER ALOYSE.]

ABBESS   Sara! The midnight hour of the Nativity is going to peal,
     filling our souls with joy! Soon the altar will be illuminated

---

* Luke xiv : 23.
** Whenever possible, Villiers' original punctuation has been retained.

7

like an Ark of Covenant! Our prayers will take flight on the wings of our carols! Before that hour joins the eternal, I must tell you the sacred decision I have made for your future.

Remember this, Sara. When your father and mother knew that death was near, they summoned me to their manor and committed you to my care. For seven years, free as a child in a garden, you have lived in this cloister. However, the games of children were always strange to you, and I have never seen you smile. What can so studious and solitary a nature mean? Will your incessant reading of all our old books ever humble your spirit?

Listen to me, Sara, you are a dark soul. On your face, ever pale, a trace of some ancient pride glimmers. It sleeps within . . . oh! the harmonies that you improvise on the organ have betrayed you! . . . They are so very gloomy that I have had to ask Sister Aloyse to play in your stead.—Despite the reserve and simplicity of your rare speech and of all your acts, I have meditated over you long and attentively. I feel that I do not know you. You submit to the discipline of our rule with sullen indifference.—Take care that you do not grow hardhearted!

My daughter, you are a lamp in a tomb; I want to revive your flame for Hope. What vanity life is without prayer! The twenty-third year of your life has passed; only unction could succour you,—with unction you would belong wholly to God, who calms anxious hearts! I admit that by the laws of men, I ought to grant that you are free to leave us; but by the laws of God, how can I, who have the charge of your soul, let you return to the world?—You would be alone, rich, beautiful in the midst of worldly temptations (which, as I am certainly not unaware, seduce violently before they fatally disenchant). Have I the right, when you have been committed to my care, not to act in this instance for the fulfillment of your real happiness since you are incapable of discerning it? Sensual experience leads to despair. Later, despite your will, you would lack the strength to reform. I must look out for you. What! If vertigo awaited you at the brink of an abyss, would I not have the right to hold you back? My failure to act would be a treacherous weakness, and you could call me to account on Judgment Day.—Not to restrain you when you want to plunge into darkness! without either spiritual director or family guardian! and with the ardent mind that I divine beneath your lowered lids? No! no. Outside, you would not know how to live in His Steps.—Therefore, I am going to offer you to Him this very evening. Yes, tonight.

[*A pause.*]

Daughter, when I broached this subject to you three months ago, you rejected it. I have had recourse to *in pace,* severe privations, mortifications . . . And while you submitted to your penance, and with resignation, moreover, I had prayers offered for you, and I myself interceded fervently, offering my tears to Him who is all forgiveness.

Do not compel me to have further recourse to these rigorous measures to make you come to yourself and to drive you, so to speak, towards Heaven. Today, on this beautiful holy evening, I have released you from your cell; I have chosen this blessed night for consecrating you to the Lord in the midst of flowers, candles, and incense. You, the betrothed *dolorosa* of this bridal night.

Thus will grace descend upon you; oblivion will make your spirit less anxious; you will feel soon the weight of divine love; and one day (perhaps it is not far off!), trembling at the memory of this holy hour, you will kiss me, your cheeks bathed in tears of ecstasy and joy.—And this will be that touching act of witness seen only by the virgins who stay in the altar shadows. And then you will understand what I have dared to do, what I have taken upon myself to carry out. Thus, may the Lord bring you peace.

[*She turns around.*]

—Sister Laudation, light the tapers.

[*During the end of this scene, the altar gradually lights up.*]

Now, my sister and daughter, as I have told you:—you are rich in this world's goods. When we enter here, we give up all pride and all wealth. We are poor; but what we have we give away, for charity alone ennobles poverty.

9

Your family has bequeathed to you castles, palaces, forests, and plains. Here is the deed by which you abandon all your goods to the community. Here is a pen. Sign.

[SARA *unfolds her arms, takes the pen, and signs impassively.*]
Fine. That is a splendid thing to do.

[*She looks at* SARA *who has resumed her immobility.*]
Thank you.

[*To herself while turning towards the* ARCHDEACON.]
May God see me—and judge me!

[*After reaching the old priest, she touches his shoulder and bends over to whisper a few words.*]

ARCHDEACON [*rising, in an undertone*] Fasting, a dark cell, and silence bring light into these proud souls; it had to be—and always shall be.

[*Aloud, coming towards* SARA.]
Sara, Sister Emmanuele in God! Whatever doubts made us suspect an evil spirit hovering around you have been dispelled. Indeed, it is true that on such a day we should have dispelled every uneasy thought about you; but the alms God lets you make us completely purifies you in our eyes from any suspicion of indifference. The gift will militate for you in moments of abandonment and dereliction. Presently I shall receive you among those from henceforth your sisters. For a long time you have been considered by them, and by us, to be both called and chosen. Your novitiate is at an end.

ABBESS Daughter, as a symbol of the marriage to come, we are going to clothe you in the bridal gown and crown you with the diadem of the holy virgins. Then you will come here where we are now during the canticles. Here you will prostrate yourself as a sign of death; and over you will be cast the pall of our dead. Beneath this flagstone rests the Blessed One who founded this convent; before the offertory you will pray especially to her. Once the vows are pronounced, your worldly hair will fall beneath the scissors of our rule. Then we shall clothe you in the holy habit which you will wear until your days of trial here below come to an end.

[*A young nun with a charming childlike face appears in blue and*

10

white vestments behind the altar. She has just grown pale. She watches Sara.]

As for me, I shall leave soon for my eternity; you will inherit my ivory crosier and you will do in your turn ... what I am doing now.

[*Turning around.*]

Come, Sister Aloyse!

[*The nun approaches.*]

SCENE 2

[*The same,* SISTER ALOYSE.]

ABBESS [*continuing*]   Sister Aloyse, here is your companion, your favourite tenderly beloved sister who is our cherished daughter. Your voice will be sweeter to her than mine, and I count on your good words to dispel the temptations which could rise in her heart at this supreme hour.

[*A pause.*]

—You love her dearly, don't you?

SISTER ALOYSE [*gravely*]   Yes, Mother.

ABBESS   I commit her to your pure and tender love. You shall keep watch and pray together in the oratory until the quarter hour before midnight.

[*The* ABBESS *mounts the steps of the pulpit stairway to the* ARCHDEACON. *The priest is now looking through some parchments and papers by the light of a lamp which* SISTER LAUDATION *has just placed on the arms of a stall.*]

SISTER ALOYSE   Dear God!

[*Clasping her hands on* SARA'S *shoulder, and in a very low, almost inaudible voice.*]

Sara, do you remember our roses along the passage of the tombs?* You came to me like a sister beyond all my hopes. To me you are next to God. I will die if you want me to. Remember at dusk when I used to rest my forehead on your

---

* Sister Aloyse uses "tu"; the others have been using "vous".

11

pale hands. I am inconsolable because I have seen you. Alas! you are the beloved! . . . You have plunged me in dejection. I have strength only to come to you.

[*A pause.*]

Yield ; become one of us beneath the veil! Share the brief earthly trial. You surely know that we cannot live! So soon we should be together in the same Heaven with a single soul! . . . Sara, see the starry Heaven in the depths of my eyes : — there extend skies forever bestarred! — Yield and come! I want to adorn you myself to be a divine bride, an ineffable spouse, a celestial being. Sorrow has given me charm, and you will no longer push me sadly away when you look at me. What more can I say to persuade you? Sara, Sara!

[*Without speaking,* SARA *unfolds her arms ; she rests her forehead on the novice's. The latter takes her hand. Both cross the sanctuary. In a choked voice, still lower,* SISTER ALOYSE, *startled.*]

Oh! don't rest your brow on mine! my knees are giving way!

[SARA *has straightened up and supports* SISTER ALOYSE *with one hand. The latter has become as white as her veil. Both slowly leave by the lateral apse.*]

ABBESS [*standing against a pillar, pensively follows them with her eyes*] It has happened! The child is succumbing already to the rapture and intoxication of hell! Seduction by the angels of darkness! Sara's excessive, dangerous beauty brings that chosen heart anxiously, distressingly to the brink of sin.

[*Reflectively.*]

Sister Aloyse shall cut Sara's hair tonight; She shall remain thus, disfigured and unveiled, until Epiphany.

ARCHDEACON [*coming towards her*] Sister, here are the patrimonial titles of Sara de Maupers and the actions which concern her; they are going to become convent property; the wealth they represent will supplement the modicum of our revenue. Take them; tomorrow you shall send them to the steward.

SCENE 3

[ABBESS, ARCHDEACON, *then* SISTER LAUDATION.]

ABBESS [*indifferently, taking up the parchments*] I thank you,
   Father.
[*Just as she is about to roll them together and tie them, her glance
becomes more attentive.*]
   These coats of arms! . . . Haven't I seen them before?—The
   oriental escutcheon which these unwonted golden sphinxes
   support . . . And this ducal crest . . .
[*Bending over, she examines the titles near the lamp.*]
   Azure—a winged Death's Head, argent, upon a septenary of
   stars of the same, in abyss ; with the device running through the
   letters of the name: *Macte Animo ! Ultima PERfulget Sola.**
   Prophetic words, if God wills; isn't Sara the last heiress of the
   Princes of Maupers?—But . . . these precious stones, or gems,
   of divers tinctures, encircling the Death's Head in chief, are
   illegible in heraldic; I cannot understand . . .
ARCHDEACON [*approaching*] You wish to decipher the blazon of
   this house? To be sure, it is more than strange, for it has seen
   seven centuries. Just so, I was going through the legend behind
   it a little while ago. It is indeed the escutcheon of the De
   Maupers family which, even more surprisingly, shares it with
   a certain German branch of an eminent Austro-Hungarian
   house, the Counts of Auersperg,—an illustrious family tree with
   numerous branches!
ABBESS [*starting*] Auersperg! . . . And . . . nothing, in that
   history could have bearing on the subject of Sara's patrimony?
ARCHDEACON [*smiling*] Nothing seems to. It's simply a romance of
   chivalry and crusades in which fairy tale gets the better of
   fact. It is this: the heads of these two families, it appears,
   were at the same time ambassadors, one from France, the other
   from Germany, at the court of a sultan (Sultan El Kalab,
   according to the chronicle of the epoch).—Now a magus, who
   aided the secret council of the Egyptian prince, was able to

---

* Courage ! Alone, the last [heiress] blazes forth !

13

persuade the two knights to exchange the pair of lions supporting their common escutcheon for these mysterious golden
sphinxes. The device of the house of Auersperg is more incom-
prehensible: *AltiUs rEsurgeRe SPERo Gemmatus!** Let's
leave these vain traditions at that.—Shouldn't the member-
elect be readied for the taking of the veil? You have been sure
to instruct her thoroughly in the ritual of our liturgy for her
consecration, haven't you?

ABBESS [*preoccupied, interrupting*] Mademoiselle de Maupers is
getting ready for the ceremony, yes, Father.

[*A pause; then, as if yielding suddenly to an inner obsession.*]
Before the divine office, let me have your lights on a series
of special circumstances which keep haunting my memory.—
These circumstances have led me to form a theory . . . of such
an extraordinary kind . . . that I hesitate in this case to take
the presentiment for certitude on my own authority; I need
your opinion. It concerns Sara.—Father, this girl, tall and
white like a Paschal taper, for us is a closed heart which holds
many things.

ARCHDEACON I, too, am wary of the stubborn lamb. At the same
time I believe that in the long run convent rule will reduce—
will lead back to us, I should say—this untamed child; yes, I
hope that with grace and commitment to God, all will go well.
—But pray be clear, is her conduct essentially at fault?

ABBESS She is too coldly exemplary. I have often punished her
to try her constancy. She has accepted everything, but, I tell
you Father, her submission is only external. Chastisement
blunts its edge upon her and confirms her in her pride.

[*Interrupting herself, as if talking to herself.*]
This girl is like steel, which bends to its centre, then stretches
out or breaks; she has (if I may use such an expression) the
soul of a sword. And more than once the sight of her has
disturbed even me with a kind of mysterious anguish.

ARCHDEACON Has she ever attempted to escape from the priory?

ABBESS [*shaking her head*] She can sense that she is observed

---

* Bejeweled, I [the heir] hope to rise higher again!

14

vigilantly night and day; an attempt to escape would subject her to more rigorous confinement.

ARCHDEACON [*looking at her closely, after a pause*] In this kind of judgment we must also be on guard ourselves against speaking under the devil's sway!—That is, it would be wise to warn Sister Emmanuele of the measures taken concerning her, that's all.

ABBESS [*smiling coldly and distantly*] Under the sway of the demon? . . . Well! Father, judge for yourself. Here are the facts in their exact sequence. I find them . . . sombre.

[*She sits down in a stall and rests her elbows on its arms ; meditates a few moments ; then, she speaks slowly, raising her eyes to the* ARCHDEACON *who stands facing her.*]

You know, a very ancient sect of Rosicrucians occupied this abbey during a war over three centuries ago. They left on the upper floors divers works on, presumably, Tyrian dialects, forgotten idioms that people used to speak at Gaza and Tadmor,—or somewhere . . . We have preserved these documents as curiosities.—Now, first of all, isn't it remarkable that I have often come upon Sara plunged in patient study of these works?—Ah! I pray, note this point well; it may become interesting in a moment.

ARCHDEACON [*first smiling, then darkening*] The fact is that she would have better meditated her Lauds. Furthermore, these books are far from being the true wisdom . . . You must have them destroyed by fire—tomorrow at the latest. In order to escape the stake the Rosicrucians used to conceal abominable formulas within ostensible prayers . . .

ABBESS These books at present—but indeed belatedly—are in my cell.—Now, one winter morning three years ago,—it was the Candlemas Eve watch, I remember,—I went down into the library rather early; there I found this astonishing girl. She had spent the night there all alone despite the rigorous cold. She did not see me come in; she did not see me watching her! . . . She was just finishing burning in her lamp the first sheet of a dusty missal, the first parchment sheet of that gothic Book of Hours with enamel covers, which once was sent to us from

Germany by a correspondent of his Highness Patriarch Pol, our pious bishop.

ARCHDEACON Yes . . . I remember . . . by a physician in Hungary, whom the Patriarch himself did not know and had never seen:—Doctor . . . Janus.

[*The septuple flames around the sanctuary lamp throw a very sharp light, then die out all at once.*]

ABBESS [*calling*] Sister Laudation! . . . Quickly!—The lamp! the lamp! . . . What can have caused this?—You will lead the Confiteor in the refectory!

[SISTER LAUDATION *runs up with clasped hands.*]

SISTER LAUDATION [*distressed and bewildered*] Mother, I forgot to fill it this evening! That's true! And this has never happened since I have had the keys on my cincture.

[*She relights the lamp silently; then she retires behind the altar.*]

ARCHDEACON You were saying then, Sister, that Sara destroyed that parchment?

SCENE 4

[ARCHDEACON, ABBESS *alone.*]

ABBESS Father, do you recall something of the sheet I am speaking of? It was covered with strangely formed characters, to which we paid slight attention since we could not translate them.

ARCHDEACON That's right, a pious invocation, no doubt.

ABBESS Those characters resembled quite uncannily those explained in the Rosicrucian books!—The parchment was superadded in the missal and stamped with the seal of these two coats of arms.

[*She points to the deeds.*]

ARCHDEACON [*after a pause*] I still do not make out your line of thought very well. Continue, Sister. How is this insignificant act . . . even laudable to a certain extent . . . ?

ABBESS [*staring into space and as if speaking to herself*] Sara's features at that moment radiated mysterious joy, a profound

16

and terrible joy. No, what she had just read was not a prayer! . . . Her expression had something solemn, unknown, unforgettable.—Taking her unawares, I questioned her, watching her eyes carefully.—The glance that she raised slowly on me was so expressionless that it gave me a feeling of danger. After a pause—and an impressive paling—she replied that she had simply just destroyed a vain memento of pride . . . her own coat of arms, which she recognized on that page.—Suspect fervour!—I reread the Patriarch's letter to assure myself of the truth. The book really did come from the deceased chatelaine of Auersperg,—and this would seem now to explain Sara's words. . . However, Father, I have retained, I admit it, from that moment which lasted but a flash, yes, I have retained a certain intuition . . . oh! a confused thought, superstition, perhaps.—But I cannot get it out of my mind! . . . This suspicion I have of Sara, this alone can give us the key to her impenetrable, grave, icy nature. Haven't you often seen her walk beneath the cloister arches, preoccupied, seemingly lost in some silent dream? I have.

ARCHDEACON [*looking at her closely*] You think that this girl? . . .

ABBESS [*her expression darkening*] Yes, it is my inner conviction. I think that Sara de Maupers has deciphered some occult clue, some strange piece of information,—a hint . . . a soverign hint! an important secret, yes, Father! yes, I tell you, a considerable secret undoubtedly!—buried in that sheet which she destroyed.

ARCHDEACON [*after a pause*] Tell me, won't the doors for the public be securely bolted this evening?

ABBESS The iron bars of the church portal are already bolted. The nave will remain empty. The sailors and hamlet folk will hear midnight mass in town.

ARCHDEACON Good, once the vows are pronounced, you will have to exercise extreme surveillance over her.

ABBESS [*in a low voice*] But, come now! . . . I believed, I had to believe that her soul was not so hidden to you! Doesn't she accuse herself when on her knees in your tribunal . . .

ARCHDEACON [*interrupting her*] On this I cannot answer you; let us speak of what we know. The vows bestow special grace, and we see that she greatly needs it. I have good reason to fear that for her the macerations will be, in a certain respect, a necessity . . .

ABBESS [*calmly*] Of course, we must save her! from herself! And if she has some infernal tare in her heart, we must uproot it for her salvation!—And consider too, Father, how powerful her charm is! I requested our youngest conversa, Sister Aloyse, who has a simple heart and an angelic soul, to seek out Sara's company.—I was hoping thus to catch, sooner or later, some heedless remark . . . a clue to her alarming motives.—What happened? Something unexpected, improbable.—The face, the extraordinary beauty of Mademoiselle de Maupers have deeply fascinated Sister Aloyse; she is now secretive, nearly lost.

ARCHDEACON [*trembling*] Be careful!—this comes from ancient enchantments! The impure fevers of Earth and Blood emit dismal mists which thicken the air of the soul and hide the face of God absolutely, suddenly.—Fasting and prayer are sometimes powerless! . . . It is a dangerous thing, a dangerous thing.

[*Shivering.*]

—Horrors!

ABBESS [*coldly*] Father, I have warded off other perils. While you celebrate over Sara the Office of the Dead tonight, her caution at the Interrogation will be this very Sister Aloyse; I have chosen her for the Penitent-Interpreter.—As for your homily, you can speak to Sara, Father, as if you had to strike the heart and mind of some unfathomable unbeliever!—Strike the mind especially! Hers, I believe, is of the most abstract, profound kind! . . . My flock of white souls will not understand you; so, there is no risk of scandal.—She alone will follow you, easily, I am sure, into those abysses of introspection which are only too familiar to her.

ARCHDEACON [*very much surprised and with a slight smile*] What? please explain! What *are* you saying?—Do you mean that?

ABBESS Ah! if I dared reveal . . . my entire thought! If I added that her very extensive knowledge, which I have divined many a

18

time in her precise, brief answers, has let me know too late that when I thought I was letting her play at reading, her extraordinary understanding had grasped by itself even the arcana of all that erudition—hidden up there in those thousands of works!

ARCHDEACON [*now thoughtful*] Truly a secretive orphan if so many books could tempt her and lead her astray!

ABBESS Take what I tell you seriously: I believe her endowed with the terrible gift Intelligence.

ARCHDEACON [*gravely*] Then, let her tremble, unless she become a saint! Revery has lost so many souls!—Especialy in a woman, this gift more often becomes a torch than a beacon . . . It is settled, let her read no more until her faith, clearly reaffirmed, will shed light on the nothingness of those human pages. You ought to have explained this trait to me earlier. I see that I must resign myself to eloquence in my homily of exhortation this evening. Young minds, darkened by precocious meditations are susceptible to the tinsel of mortal languages.—Eloquence! As if it was not dirt underfoot for those who can say the Lord's Prayer! And as if, for example, the dazzling saying of Saint Paul: *Omnis Christianus Christus est,** needed ornament or vain glosses, when it expresses God! Alas! I understand good Chrysotom and his tears of pity, of shame, too undoubtedly, when he beheld his faithful followers admiring his words like spectators at the theatre— the physical harmony, the brilliant covering, the sensual beauty, the phraseology—instead of taking in their substantial sense! How he used to implore God to forgive them and himself for this scandalous mockery! Wretchedness! A good lashing for discipline, long and humble prayers, good privations and good fasts, this is what gives substance to our faith, this is what is worth something, what counts at Death, this is what creates a claim, solidifying our supernatural element.—In short! if eloquence is necessary to persuade that imperilled soul . . .

---

* Every Christian is Christ. Either the author or the character is absentminded here: it was Angelus Silesius, *Cherubinischer Wandersmann*, V, 7, who said, "All the blessed are one and every Christian is Christ".

[*Disdainfully.*]

    I shall have it this evening—yes, once the circle of pedantic quotations of holy scholasticism is exhausted, I shall dare on my own to combat as a rhetorician her sinful indecision,—but not forgetting meanwhile those clairvoyant words of the Psalmist: *Quoniam non cognovi litteraturam, introibo in potentias Dei.**

ABBESS However, I ought to believe her well disposed! Perhaps she tries to pray!—See, she has just renounced her earthly goods and signed them into my hands.

ARCHDEACON [*looking at the act of donation*] Ho! I was forgetting! that's right. How many poor people to feed! by the hundreds! How many pilgrims to comfort! . . . Yes, perhaps efficient grace has touched her! perhaps we are tormented by one of those unwarranted suspicions, sent by the spirits of Evil on solemn occasions to arouse our weakness!

ABBESS How many beds for the sick! How much white bread and fortifying wine! How much good can be done with this gold snatched from Mammon!

ARCHDEACON [*dreamily*] The weapons of the Most Evil One will turn against him! Then, peace be with us!

[*Both kneel before the altar; then, raising their arms towards Heaven.*]

ABBESS and ARCHDEACON [*in unison forcefully*] Glory to God of the distressed, who inspired the Samaritan!

[*Bells.—The altar is now illuminated, and its reflections cover the whole enclosure.*]

CHOIR OF NUNS [*outside, walking and singing*] *O virgo! mater alma! fulgida Cœli porta!/Te nunc flagitant devota corda et ora,/Nostra ut pura pectora sint et corpora!***

[*The cloister door opens; the NUNS, radiant and serene in white*

---

* " Because I did not study literature, I shall enter God's power ". Perhaps he refers to Psalm lxxi: 15-16: " for I know not the numbers *thereof*. I will go in the strength of the Lord God ".

    ** O virgin! dear mother! shining gate of Heaven!
      Now our devout hearts and mouths entreat you,
      That our hearts and bodies be pure!

*vestments, enter the hemicycle of the stalls.—An old man in the
surplice of an acolyte comes to the approaches of the altar and
places himself at the right corner of the first step.]*

SCENE 5

[ARCHDEACON, ABBESS, SISTER LAUDATION, CELEBRANT OF THE
OFFICE OF THE DEAD, NUNS.]

[Organ music. The four rows of stalls are now filled. Two NUNS
*in festal robes approach the altar, take the censers and cast
incense into them. Others, standing upon the steps with baskets in
their hands, scatter handfuls of flower petals on the parvis; the*
ABBESS, *holding the white crosier, is seated in her abbatial chair.
She has just donned a sparkling cope. A canticle rises. The*
ARCHDEACON, *vested in a black stole, approaches; the minister
kneels. The golden bell rings. It is the Introit.]*

A NUN [*in solo*] *In te, Domine, speravi : non confundar in
æternum.*

CHOIR *Amen.*

ARCHDEACON *Judica me, Deus, et discerne causam meam de gente
non sanctà! . . .**

*[After a brief pause, he mounts the steps to the Tabernacle. The
preliminaries of the lucernal mass cont'nue in hushed voices while
awaiting midnight. Soon the offertory bell rings; all the* NUNS *rise.]*

SCENE 6

[*The same,* SARA *and* SISTER ALOYSE.]

[The organ swells. SARA *appears, clothed in a long white moiré
tunic, the sacred opal necklace on her breast. She rests her hand on
the shoulder of* SISTER ALOYSE, *who is pale and smiling. Orange
blossoms are twined in her abundant unbound hair which ripples in*

---

* I have hoped in you, Lord: I shall not be damned in eternity.
Judge me, God, and separate my cause from the unholy people.

black and scattered waves upon her gown. Her face is almost marmorean. When she comes into sight, flowers are thrown before her; the censers are raised.]

[*She comes to the altar and kneels silently upon the blessed flagstone; then she lies at full-length, her forehead on her folded arms.*]

[SISTER ALOYSE *drapes over her a vast white cloth laden with spots of gold, representing enormous tears, and covers her entirely.*]

[*On the first step of the altar the mystic taper burns above* SARA'S *forehead.*]

ARCHDEACON [*standing on the parvis and turning toward those present*] Is there a soul here who wishes to crucify her mortal life by binding herself forever to the divine sacrifice I am going to offer?

SISTER ALOYSE [*advancing*]   *Ego pro defuncta illa! Ego vox ejus!*
[*Standing by* SARA *and chanting the litany of consecration.*]
   Suscipe me, Deus! secundum eloquium tuum, et vivam!

CELEBRANT OF THE OFFICE OF THE DEAD   *Si iniquitatas observaveris, Domine, Domine quis sustinebit!*

NUNS [*passing in procession around* SARA *with lighted tapers in their hands*]   *Requiescat, et ei luceat perpetua Lux!*

SISTER ALOYSE [*after sprinkling holy water upon the pall*]   *Resurgam.*

NUNS [*distant voices in the organ loft*]   *In excelsis.**

CHOIR [*on stage*]   *Amen.*

[*Now the old acolyte still on the parvis of the altar has vested the* ARCHDEACON *in the insignia under which former high Priors of the abbey could receive vows in the name of the Pope. His long black cope pinned with clasps to his shoulders, his diaconal mitre on his brow, the* ARCHDEACON *stands under the purple-black dias, embroidered with golden ossments, held by four of the abbey's*

---

* I speak for the dead! I am her voice!
  Lord, catch me up! One word from you and I shall live!
  If you O Lord shall mark iniquities, who can stand?
  May she rest and may perpetual light shine upon her!
  I shall rise!
  Glory in the highest.

oldest mother tutrices. He goes down to SARA, *still prostrate.— The organ stops.*]

ARCHDEACON If she who, already dead to the earth, lying here before the face of God, repudiates forever the wretched joys which flesh and blood can offer, let her be welcome at the foot of the altar!

SISTER ALOYSE [*pointing to* SARA *with both hands*] *Ecce ancilla Dei.**

[*At this word and during the silence which follows,* SISTER LAUDATION *at a sign from the* ABBESS, *approaches* SISTER ALOYSE *and hands her the large silver scissors.* SISTER ALOYSE *receives then and, horrified, closes her eyes.*]

ARCHDEACON [*stopping on the third step, to* SARA] Are you** truly the woman called from on High, who desires to live under the humble vows of chastity which illuminate us? she who wishes to cry to the Throne with Cecilia: *Fiat cor meum immaculatem et non confundar!*** she who in a few mortal days, couched upon the beautiful wings of death, will fly away in most holy flight, toward the spirits aflame with love and light, the *beata Seraphim* of whom pious Areopagite speaks? O woman! if you come in oblation, you offer your burning love to God: thus you will become love itself when you enter into eternity.

[*Bell of the dead.*]

Because eternity, Saint Thomas says exceedingly well, is only the full possesion of oneself in a single and same instant. And " My love is my weight! " Saint Augustine tells us. Sink down then, if you have a celestial heart, into the abyss of Him who is love itself! faith, according to the expression of Saint Paul, is the substance of things which *have to be hoped for.*****

[*Bell of the Dead.*]

By faith you will be born again, transfigured into your own hymn of joy, the soul being a harmony, as Saint Hildegard

---

* Behold the handmaiden of God.
** The Archdeacon begins to address Sara as " tu ".
*** Let my heart be made immaculate that I may not de damned!
**** Hebrews xi 1: " Now faith is the substance of things hoped for, the evidence of things not seen."

23

said with inspiration.—*Pulcher hymnus Dei homo immortalis !** Lactius said, too, a very praiseworthy and learned spirit. Hate only one thing: any obstacle to your return to God! any limitation, that is Evil! Hate it with all your strength! Because, thus as Saint Isidore of Damiette specifies admirably, the elect, leaning over the heights of heaven to contemplate the torments of the reproved, will feel an ineffable joy at the sight of their torture; without which, the fruition of divine work and the fellowship of praise of their infinite equity—which is the very *form* of Paradise—would be incomplete.

Oh! if you do not understand yet the spirit of our dogma, if your clay trembles over it, let it be permitted to you to examine it thoroughly, since God has made you so strangely studious and persevering, as if you were called to become like the great woman saints.

—*Negligentiae mihi videtur si non studemus quod credimus intelligere.*** Saint Anselm puts it felicitously. But study with humility, and, especially, with a heart that is always simple, if you want to advance in the knowledge of God.—Thus you will keep that dignity of hope, without which humility itself has no perfect value at all . . . and soon, undoubtedly, a special grace will instruct you that the unique means of understanding is prayer. Do not forget; you will never be pure spirit. Your soul itself, your imperishable soul, is composed first of *matter* in order to be able to rejoice or suffer eternally while remaining distinct from God. *Materia prima,* says the Angel of the School, seventy-fifth question . . . And remember that the bull of Clement V strikes with excommunication whoever might dare to dream the contrary!—And if, outside of intellectual obedience to the Church, your understanding revolts —and looks for God in another way, alas!—Repeat to yourself for your salvation that troubled confession of a pagan rhetorician: " Such is the vanity, the infirmity of Man's reason

---

* An immortal man is a beautiful hymn to God!

** It seems to me to be negligence if we do not study to understand what we believe.

24

that he could not conceive a God *whom he wanted to resemble !* " Learn therefore to check the pride of your deceptive reason. What other proof of God can you seek but in prayer? Is not Faith the unique proof of everything? No other proof furnished by the senses or reason would satisfy your mind, you already know that. So then, what is the good of even seeking? . . . To believe, is not that projecting oneself into the object of one's belief and realising oneself in it? Affirm, as you are affirmed : cease your pursuit, it is wiser! . . . Then having acquired by prayer the conviction of the presence of God, you will grasp the wisdom of it! You will have attained your hope in a flash.—Even yesterday when you were not, God truly believed in you, since here you are just summoned from Nothingness by creative Faith! Return to Him, therefore, the echo of His call! It is your turn to believe in Him! It is your turn to CREATE Him in you, with all the *being* of your life! You are here below not to look for " proofs ", but to bear witness whether by love and faith, you weigh the weight of salvation.

[*Bell of the dead.*]

Listen once more, while the bell of the dead rings for you.— If any of the Three Mysteries, divine principles, did not appear as if it were impossible and absurd to our eyes of clay and pride, what merit would we have in believing in it? And, if they were possible and reasonable, would you accept them as divine, since you, dust that you are, could encompass them by a thought? If therefore they are absurd and impossible, they are precisely what they must be, and, as Tertullian instructs, it is in that way first that they present the first guarantee of their truth : their human absurdity is the sole luminous point which renders them accessible to our ephemeral logic under the condition of Faith. Therefore, purify your soul forever of this tare of pride which alone separates it from the sight of God; cease to be human; be divine. The world treats us as madmen who delude themselves so far as to sacrifice their days to a puerile dream, to the shadow of an imagined heaven.—But what man, his final hour come, does not realise that he has wasted his life in bitter dreams, never fulfilled, in vanities which deceived him in successive disillusions, which, indeed, probably had reality only in his mind? From thence what gives the world the right to be so presumptuous when indeed it pleases us to prefer knowingly the sublime dream of God to the mortal lies of earth? . . . Mark this! Our hearts are warmed. Our peace of mind is deepened, fearing no dangers. Heaven, already perceived, penetrates us from here on with blessed love; prayer becomes a vision for us;—exegesis, the very key of Evidence . . . And the children of the century in the name of the dolorous ennui, brought on by the deceptive realities of the senses, dare to call our positive happiness imaginary?—Let them stand back!

[*Smiling.*]

Illusion for illusion, we keep *that* of God, who alone gives to his dazzled eternal children joy, light, strength, and peace. No creature, no vitality escapes Faith. Man prefers one belief to another. And for him who doubts, if only in the vague forms of thought, the doubt, which he admits freely into his mind, is still only a form of Faith, since in principle doubt is as mysterious as our mysteries. Only the man who is uncommitted stays with his irresolution which becomes the null sum of his life. He thinks that he " analyses ". He digs the grave of his soul and returns to a nothingness which now can only be called Hell.—Because for non-existence it is always too late. We are irrevocable.

[*Bell of the Dead.*]

—Yes, Faith envelopes us! The universe is only its symbol. We *must* think. We *must* act. We are constrained to this slavery: thinking. Doubting thought is still obeying it. There is no act which is not created by an instinctive thought! not a thought which is not blind in its primordial idea! Indeed, since we can become only our thoughts united to the occult flesh of our acts, let us think and act so that a God can grow within us!—and do this first of all! if we want to acquire faith, if we want to *merit* having it.

All speculation controverting the growth of our soul in God

26

is *time lost,* which the Saviour alone can redeem.—Everything STRIVES around us! The grain of wheat, which rots in darkness in the soil, does it *see* the sun? No, but it has faith. That is why it climbs, by and through death, towards the light. Thus with the chosen seeds of anything, with the exception of seeds of disbelief, where Doubt sleeps with its impurities and scandals, and being indifferent, totally die. *We* are the wheat of God; we feel that we shall be born again in Him,— who is, according to the enlightened and magnificent axiom of a theologian, the place of spirits just as space is the place of bodies.*

[*Bell of the dead.*]

Believe in hope and prayer! with the heart full of love! such is our doctrine. And even when, as the council warns us, through the impossible, an angel of heaven should come to teach us another doctrine, we should persist, firm and unshakable, in our faith.

[*A pause.*]

—Now, Eve Sara Emmanuele, Princess of Maupers, heeding the power of the words sworn before those who represent the Lord, those of the INJUNCTION by which the Word becomes flesh, pronounce, therefore, of your own free will, the supreme vows which commit your soul.**

CHOIR OF NUNS   *Ecce inviolata soror cœlestis!*

ARCHDEACON [*continuing and alternating with the choir*] . . . Your blood, your being, in this world and the next.

CHOIR OF NUNS   *Ecce conjux!*

ARCHDEACON   . . . your unique and infinite hope.

CHOIR OF NUNS   *Sacra esto!****

ARCHDEACON   Sara! your betrothal ring gleams on this altar.****

---

* Malebranche said this.

** The Archdeacon now addresses Sara as "vous".

*** Behold the inviolate celestial sister!
    Behold the bride!
    That she be holy!

**** The Archdeacon uses "tu".

I love God; that means " God loves me ", I say unto you!
. . . Love therefore and *afterwards do what you please !* Saint
Augustine cried.—Sara, do you hear these voices, already
celestial, which call you? . . . One word, and I shall raise
my right hand over your forehead to absolve you,—and,
consecrated to the Light forever, you will be joined to the
Bridegroom in Heaven! Then, before the woman reborn, the
Office of mourning, being transformed into a mass of glory,
will conclude in the midnight joy of the Good Tidings! And
the lilies of your vows will be scattered by the Angels upon
the crèche of the Holy Child.

[*The Bell of the dead strikes quickly three times, then stops.*]
—But . . . the twenty-third ring of that bell, counting the
years of your mortal existence, cautions me to leave you
alone with your soul during the supreme instant when you
must ponder only the Irrevocable Judgment.

[*Having entrusted his pastoral crosier to the Celebrant kneeling
on his right, he climbs to the Tabernacle to take the Holy Chrism.*]

CELEBRANT OF THE OFFICE OF THE DEAD [*reciting in monotone the
text of Saint Bernard,* Preparation for the Last Judgment.]
*Attende, homo, quid fuisti antè ortum et quod eris usque ad
occasum. Perfectò fuit quod non eras. Posteà, de vili materia
factus, in utero matris de sanguine menstruali nutritus, tunica
tua, fuit pellis secundina. Deindè, in vilissimo panno involutus,
progressus es ad nos,—sic indutus et ornatus ! Et non memor
es quæ sit origo tua. Nihil est aliud homo quam sperma
fœtidum, saccus stercorum, cibus vermium. Scienta, sapienta,
ratio, sine Deo Christo, sicut nubes transeunt.*

Post hominem vermis: post vermem fœtor et horror;

Sic, in non hominem, veritur omnis homo.

*Cur carnem tuam adornas et impiguas, quam, post paucos
dies, vermes devoraturi sunt in sepulchro, animam, verò, tuam
non adornas, quæ Deo et angelis ejus præsentenda est in
Cœlis!* *

[*A pause.*]

SISTER ALOYSE and the NUNS [*in unison*]   *Tuis autem fidelibus,* *vita mutatur, non tollitur! Et, dissolutà terrestri domo, cœlestis domus comparatur!***

[*The golden mass bell rings.*]

[*Sara uncovers her face, rises under the candelabra and puts her elbows on the first step of the altar. The opals of the mystical necklace scintillate among the incense fumes; a shower of lily petals strews the carpet around her.*]

[*In the midst of the censers and tapers she straightens up before the* ARCHDEACON. *She is now standing motionless with folded arms and lowered eyelids. On her shoulders sparkle the golden tears of the pall with the folds falling behind her and trailing over the flagstones.*]

---

* Man, hear, what you were and what you will be in the end. Surely it was what you were not. Afterwards, made of vile material, nurtured by menstrual blood in the mother's uterus, your tunic was second skin. Then, clothed in most vile garments, you have progressed to us,—thus dressed and adorned! And you are not mindful of what your origin was. Man is nothing other than fetid sperm, a sack of dung, food for worms. Science, sapience, reason without our Lord Jesus Christ pass away like the clouds.
    After man the worm: after the worm, stink and horror;
        Thus every man is turned into not-man.
Why do you adorn and paint your flesh, which after a few days in the tomb is devoured by worms, your soul, yet, you do not adorn,—which must be presented to God and his Angels in heaven!

** However, for you faithful, life is changed, not consumed! And when the terrestrial home is broken up, the home of heaven is provided!

II

The Renunciatrix

ARCHDEACON [*holding the gold grail, comes back down to her*] On this sublime night the Star of the Magi and the Shepherds rises for you also!

[*He uncovers the Holy Chrism; the* NUNS *kneel.*]
Answer! Do you accept Light, Hope and Life?

SARA [*gravely, distinctly, and gently*] No.

ARCHDEACON [*shuddering, drops the sacred vase on the altar steps where the holy oil spreads*] Lord God!

[*He recoils; his hand convulsively seizes again the gold staff of his crosier; he leans on it. Terrified, the* NUNS *leave in panic, blowing out their tapers in their disordered flight; breviaries fall here and there.—Noise of stalls abruptly deserted.—All the* NUNS, *quaking, hurriedly wrapping their large veils about them, surround the* ABBESS, *who has risen to stare at the renunciatrix. Stupefaction. Silence.* SISTER ALOYSE *has fallen, perhaps fainted, at* SARA'S *feet. All is abandoned around them—the baskets of flowers, the censers still smoking.*]

SISTER LAUDATION [*to herself, crossing herself*] Now I understand! the evil omen of the night: the lamp of God went out . . . those of the Foolish Virgins went out also before the Bridegroom!

ABBESS [*blanching, almost choking*] O night of doom!

[*Midnight strikes.—Joyful bells peal tumultuously in the distance. Carillons.*]

CHOIR OF NUNS [*hidden in the organ loft, burst forth*] Noël! Noël! Alleluia!/Hodiè contritum est, pede virgineo/Caput serpentis antiqui!*

ABBESS [*striking the flagstones with her crosier*] Stop! stop the chants!

---

* Noel! Noel! Alleluia! / Today is crushed by the virgin's foot, / The head of the ancient serpent!

31

CHOIR [*in the loft at the same time covering her voice*] *Noël,*
Alleluia! Noël!

[*The* NUNS *in the organ gallery have not seen the act which took place before the altar; and at the sound of the bells the choirs exalt the glory of the Nativity. Then, they are childless! these chosen daughters,—at the news of a little infant king of Angels just born to appease their mystical tenderness,—how could they hear voices from earth? . . . Oh! these gentle souls, forever virgin, are beside themselves!*]

CHOIR [*in the loft at the sound of the annunciation bells*] *Adeste,*
fideles! /Lœti, triumphantes! /Venite in Bethlehem! *

ABBESS [*shrieking in the midst of Alleluias while the songs continue*]
Silence! . . . Oh! this is horrible!

[*Frightened, the old Celebrant flees from the sanctuary.*]

CHOIR [*intoxicated by hymns of joy, at the sound of the organ and bells*] *Natum videte, regum Angelorum ;/Deum infantem, pannis involutum !/Venite, adoremus Dominum !*

[SISTER LAUDATION *strikes violently with her clapper ; the hymns suddenly stop; the immense serge draperies separate, revealing in the light of the pensile lamps the deserted church and the heavy-bolted entrance glimpsed between ranks of pillars, chairs and benches. Far back in the illuminated organ gallery, the choral sisters have been silenced.*]

ABBESS [*beside herself, shouting*] Be quiet! Be quiet!

[*The bells, organ, and chants have stopped.*]

ARCHDEACON [*with a dreadful sigh*] At last!

ABBESS [*horrified, pointing her cross toward the door of the stalls*]
Fly, leave this place, my daughters! Let each one of you retire
to her cell and there, prostrate in fervent orisons, implore
God's mercy! You will not hear mass tonight.—Sister Calixte,
what do we have in the treasury?

SISTER CALIXTE [*stammering after a pause*] Three hundred and
twenty-three gold pieces, twelve ecus, plus twelve sous in the
collection today.

ABBESS You will distribute all of that to the poor tomorrow.

---

* The nuns are singing " O Come all ye faithful! "

[*The door to the cloisters is opened; the* NUNS *flee and disappear like shadows.*]
[*The sisters of the precentorship have already left their tiered benches around the organ.—At present, two or three black forms, postulants, most likely, come and go in the abandoned galleries; they extinguish the tapers and close the antiphonaries. Soon, darkness effected, they withdraw also. Now all have gone down into the monastery.*]

SCENE 7

[SARA, ABBESS, ARCHDEACON, SISTER LAUDATION, SISTER ALOYSE.]

[*The* ABBESS *goes down, approaches the* ARCHDEACON, *and stands near him on the altar steps. Pointing to* SARA, *she speaks in a flat voice, choked by violent emotion.*]

ABBESS   Father, this is the act of a woman possessed. We will have to purify the church by fire tomorrow! I leave you. I am struck dumb, interdicted. The sacrilege . . . oh! the sacrilege is so very great that only infinite divine Mercy can efface it . . . What you ordain for this baneful daughter, once our companion, will be carried out.

[SISTER LAUDATION, *who has been kneeling by a pillar, rises and suddenly approaches* SARA.]

SISTER LAUDATION [*looking at her wrathfully*]   Plague-stricken wretch! . . .

[*She is going to strike* SARA'S *face; her hand already raised, stops suddenly, as if secretly immobilized.* SARA *has not even raised her eyes or trembled.*]

ABBESS   Tourière, get away from this ill-fated woman and contain your indignation in the holy sanctuary!

SISTER LAUDATION [*to herself, thoughtfully, leaving by the cloister door*]   What sudden trouble held back my arm?—Why didn't I strike?

ABBESS [*very low, to the* ARCHDEACON]   Remember especially what

33

I warned you about a little while ago: plumb this sombre heart.—The secret, father, the secret!

[*She goes down to* SISTER ALOYSE, *who is coming to, and raises her in her arms.*]

SISTER ALOYSE [*in a dying fall*] Good-bye, good-bye, Sara!

[*The* ABBESS, *staggering, half-carries, half-drags the stricken girl to the cloister door. They go out.* SISTER LAUDATION *follows them after a final sinister glance at* SARA.]

[SARA *and the* ARCHDEACON *are alone.*]

ARCHDEACON [*terrorizing*] Woman, you have been a coward. You have blushed for Him . . . who will blush for you. You have frightened souls as pure as the morning star! You have defied divine wrath, outraged the God who rescued you from nothingness and offered you His Kingdom. You call yourself Lazarus, yet you have resisted the sovereign voice which shouted to you to come out. You have refused your seat at the banquet, and refused in front of me whose task is to bring you to your seat by force. Because, just as laws incline or oblige men to duty, so can God, principle and end of all laws, all duty and force, bend and violate—miraculously—conscience and freedom.

[*A pause.*]

In the name of your salvation, for which He gave up His spirit on the inevitable Cross of that eternally mysterious mountain, I wish to see in you only a victim bewitched by the princes of Hell. What do you expect? Eviction from the monastery? No, you insensate creature, you shall not leave! —Today the authority of men would protect your escape, I know that:—you shall not escape! If at the bottom of your heart some solitary secret is hidden like a serpent in a rock, forget it, for it will be fruitless:—and it will be fruitless because you are poor, having abandoned your goods to the cause of Faith . . . as if by one last movement of divine Inspiration and Grace!—No, you shall certainly not go wandering on the roads like a human being, scattering to the winds what little remains of your soul! We are to answer for that soul, do you hear?—Do you think you are free before us, who have taught men to chastise Force and who alone know what Right consists of? What was a woman here below before Christianity? She was a slave. We have enfranchised her and delivered her . . . and you would invoke before us the word freedom as if we were not Freedom itself!—Listen and weigh my words well: Our Justice and Right do not derive from those of men. We were the ones who implanted and kindled in their essentially fratricidal intelligence these concepts of self-mastery—for their own salvation. They have forgotten, I know. So today they discuss freedom, the way they used to talk in the Tower of Babel, without being able to comprehend one another's distorted interpretation of the word. This is precisely the punishment for their ancient pride. Our supremacy on earth is the unique sanction of any law whatsoever. No person or institution can override our supremacy,—because a consequence cannot call its principle into doubt or examination,—under pain of ceasing to be a certainty itself. And any man, slave, or prince can reproach us for our food only with our bread in his mouth. We have the Authority; we hold it from God, and we will keep it in our vast hands until the consummation of centuries. And we will do that despite the threats of the future, the illusions of science, and all the foul smoke of mortal brains, so that the word will be fulfilled: *Stat Crux dùm volvitur orbis.** Let them strike us, forsake us, forget us, hate us, despise us, torture us, kill us, what of that! All that is only vanity! Fruitless rebellion. Strong with our conscience forever solid and untroubled, we will be those whom Saint Ambrose calls *Candidatus martyrum exercitus !*** Finally (and in this frightening hour this is what matters), we have a right by which the three-fold essence grants every other: thus the Son is begotten of the Father, and the Holy Spirit proceeds from the Father and the Son! And there is no other initial thought on earth as it is in Heaven.

---

* The Cross stands while the world turns.
** Candidate for the army of martyrs.

35

Therefore, Sara, since through miracle there is vested in me the power to act in this case in an efficacious and salutary manner I seize Force in the name of God to use against you, to save you from your vile nature. You shall return to the cell! You shall fast until your wretched flesh, now in revolt, shall be subdued. Your beauty is hell made manifest; your hair tempts you! your flashing eyes lead others into sin! All that must be quickly extinguished and crushed; for it is a delusion of outer darkness where all is transformed and effaced . . . I take the earthworm to witness for that. You could not see yourself such as you are at this moment without dying.—Do you imagine that Magdalen was not so beautiful? Be assured that as soon as she saw herself after her vision was illuminated by God the sublime sinner trembled with horror the rest of her life. Pray, as she prayed, to obtain what illuminates us! Let her be your example until your last sigh! And you will be our sister, our saint, our child!

[*A pause.*]

One day, if your repentance is sincere, you will come back to our midst. I doubt it; but it is my duty to hope for it . . . for divine Mercy and Love are boundless. Until then we shall pray for you day and night, in consternation, tears and fasts! —I myself in pronouncing the ritual of exorcism shall put on the cilice on your behalf.*

[*He goes down the steps. Opaque,* SARA *has not once flinched or raised her eyes.*]

ARCHDEACON But,—here is an inspiration which comes to me directly from Heaven! Under this slab the sainted founder of this ancient abbey, the blessed Apollodora, rests among the angels. This vault, the close presence of these divinely potent relics, is the very *in pace* for you. It is here that the most benign saint will intercede for you—at your side during waking and sleeping, sanctifying your bread and water, if you do these

---

* With " your behalf " the Archdeacon begins to use again the " vous " form.

things in remembrance of her.*

[*With the tip of his heavy crosier he glides open the two bolts of the vast slab, then slips the crosier through the ring. The stone, yielding to his effort, rises. The wide earthen steps of the sepulchral excavation appear; the large slab stands upright on its hinges.*]

Here is the door . . . . the *janua*** . . . . through which I rightly compel you to come into Life ; for, thus as Saint Ignatius of Loyola has spoken with profundity, " the end justifies the means "; and it is written : " Compel *them* to come in! " Come, my cherished daughter! My beloved daughter!—Go down there. Be in bliss! The alms which you have given surely entitle you to this last grace ; profit from it. Therefore, bless your trial that it may bring you satisfaction and in your turn . . . .

[*Humbly he bows before her.*]

Pray for me!

[SARA *finally raises her eyes. She looks at the priest and at the tomb which gapes near her. Mute, expressionless, she walks to a pillar. She seizes among the ex-voto offerings hung by grateful sailors, an old double axe, a guisarme ; then, deliberate, hostile yet indifferent, she walks back. At the gaping hole, she simply points a finger to the excavation and vaguely yet imperatively motions the old priest to go down into the tomb himself.*]

[*Dumbfounded, the* ARCHDEACON *recoils.* SARA *advances toward him, the axe high and sparkling now ! The old man looks around him, then looks at her. He sees that he is alone. If he opens his mouth, the fearful weapon in the calm, rebellious young fist seems ready to strike him down. He smiles bitterly and sorrowfully, shrugs his shoulders sadly.—And, perhaps to prevent a more horrible crime, he obeys* SARA *while she watches him impassively.*]

[*He covers himself with a sweeping sign of the cross and descends the steps which he strikes with his crosier and brushes with his*

---

* Here, using " en sa commémoration ", the author has either a slip or a pun. Either " commendation " or " commemoraison " is an ecclesiastical term which would apply in Sara's case.

** Outer door.

*long black cope. Little by little his gold-mitred head goes below
and disappears.*]

The voice of the ARCHDEACON *from the subterranean vault :   In te,
    Domine, speravi: non confundar in æternum.**

S C E N E   9

[SARA, *alone.*]

[SARA *throws down the axe with a gesture that makes the slab of
the vault close and with the tip of her sandal pushes each iron
bolt. Her face is expressionless. This done, she approaches the
stained-glass window and pulls the cord. The window swings
open violently. Snow and night wind blow through the church—
putting out the tapers.***]

[*Then in the darkness* SARA *tears the pall and knots the two
halves securely. An instant later, having thrown a pilgrim's garb
over her holy day vestments, she stands on the abbatial chair.
Then with a svelte, vigorous leap, she seizes one of the iron
bars with one hand and with a spring hoists herself onto the
window sill.*]

[*Next she glides between the bars onto the outside sill and looks
out below, into space, distance, infinity.*]

[*Outside the night—dreadful, dark, starless. Winds blow and
roar. Snow falls.*]

[SARA *turns around, attaches the twisted, torn pall to a bar, tries
the knot, covers her head with the gray cowl of her habit,—then
lowers herself and disappears outside, out of sight, suspended
silently in the glacial, snow-filled night.*]

---

* In you, Lord, have I hoped : may I not be damned in eternity.
** Another author's slip. The postulants have already extinguished the tapers.

PART II
THE TRAGIC WORLD

quia nominor leo.*

Phædre

*. . . because I am called a lion.

I

Watchmen of the Sovereign Secret

[*A lofty hall with an oak ceiling. An iron candelabrum hangs from the centre of the intersecting beams. In the rear the wide main entrance opens onto a vestibule. This doorway is crowned by the Auersperg escutcheon supported by its large gold sphinxes.*]

[*At left a large gothic window discloses a view of immense, mist-covered forests on the horizon.*]

[*At right a stone stairway is built into the wall; at the top of the stairs an arched doorway leads to one of the towers.*]

[*It is already deep twilight.*]

[*The depth of the hall gives the impression of a colossal pile dating from the early years of the middle ages.—At right in the vast fireplace an immense fire lights the stage. Dusty folios are piled upon the spacious mantel of this hearth.—On adjacent wide black wood shelves alembics, astral spheres, antique clay lamps, heaps of bones of extinct animals, and dried herbs are piled in disorder.*]

[*On the walls are hung war trophies, oriental oriflammes, and very old portraits of German chatelaines and higher barons. Amidst the suits of Saracen armour are nailed enormous vultures and tawny eagles with wings extended.*]

[*In the foreground doors at right and left; hangings and tapestries of high warp hang over the doors.*]

[*In the middle of the hall a table is laid for a banquet; fox skins and black bearskins lie at the feet of the old-fashioned chairs facing each other at either end of the table.*]

[*A tall old man, seated near the fireplace, examines the arms which he has just polished. He is wearing a brown wool surcoat held by a leather sword belt and old cavalry trousers of the same material and shade. He wears a Prussian beret on his thin, brush-cut white hair. He wears the Iron Cross on his chest.*]

SCENE 1

[MIKLAUS *alone.*]

MIKLAUS There!—These carabines and hunting knives... all
shining; the flask is full of kirsh; wolves beware!
[*He rises and looks around.*]
    Ah! night has fallen.
[*He goes to the window and peers into the darkness.*]
    How the wind blows out there in the pines! the heather
bends low, the bats don't fly; signs of a wind-storm. We had
better secure the casement windows. The smell of pitch may be
healthful in the daytime, but it is unhealthy at night,—
especially at the approach of spring.

SCENE 2

[MIKLAUS, HARTWIG and GOTTHOLD *entering from the left.*]
[*These tall old men built with rather noble bearing like* MIKLAUS
still wear half-military clothing; they too have the Iron Cross.]

GOTTHOLD Miklaus, it is time to light the torchières for the two
diners.
MIKLAUS [*coming downstage, rubbing his hands*] And the fire too
because you can feel the last winter winds!
[*He goes to the fireplace and makes the fire blaze again.*]
    So, the doctor still will not come down for supper?
HARTWIG [*shivering*] No.—Brr! don't spare the pine knots; make
that really blaze!—Oh! the stones make this room so humid!
—The other wing of the castle is not so bleak, or so it seems
to me. Here you're cold; and it's peculiar; outside it's warm,
even close,—an old sign that a severe storm is on the way.
GOTTHOLD [*shivering also, looking around*] It's because here the
wind comes through the green ivy on the granite outside.
Yes, this room is freezing.
MIKLAUS [*who piles enormous logs in the hearth*] Also, why is it
never used except on ceremonial occasions? Only Master Janus
comes in here sometimes . . .

42

[GOTTHOLD *lights the candelabra.* MIKLAUS, *rising, considers the lights reflected on the stone walls and woodwork, on the peeling gilt crescents of the standards. The blue shimmerings of the fire on the long swords, cimiters and daggers, the eyes of birds of prey, the vermillion angles of the picture frames, and the barrels of the arquebuses and carabines, all scatter mirrored reflections which animate the faces in the old portraits.*]

MIKLAUS What deterioration! Just look at the paintings! The hard features of the Rhinegraves and the beautiful brows of the chatelaines in Lord Axel's family are effaced; the tapestries have lost their patterns.

HARTWIG And look at this gold damascened brass armour conquered in the first crusade by Prince Elcias of Auersperg, knight of Germany, from the Saracen Emir Saharil the first. It is entirely eaten with rust, and the dead wood of the lance has broken off because of the dampness.

MIKLAUS Ah! I am not anxious to polish them; it's haunted in here!

[*The three veterans, now standing around the white tablecloth and lighted candles, appear illuminated against the confused background of shadows cast by the vaulting of the room. Their faces are energetic and tense; advanced age and sedentary occupations in the fortress have not dimmed their steady gaze. A terrible scar furrows* GOTTHOLD'S *face from top to bottom;—and the left sleeve of* HARTWIG'S *heavy military jacket hangs from the shoulder with the empty cuff sewn upon his chest; while on the right side of* MIKLAUS' *forehead a bullet has hollowed an impression.*]

[*And truly around them in the atmosphere of the hall an impression of extraordinary solemnity reigns; undoubtedly they succumb to it while trying not to think too much about it; still it heightens their speech and their silence.*]

GOTTHOLD [*to* MIKLAUS] Do you know that the Commander is going to leave?—Otto, his servant, set out this very morning with his master's baggage . . . and from here to the Prussian frontier, is far!

MIKLAUS What! this brilliant lord returns without even having seen Doctor Janus?

GOTTHOLD Yes. Tonight. It's the farewell banquet. Here are pretty tufts of rosemary and an armful of verbena, woodroses, and mint. Put them between the candelabra for me; flowers give a festive air. Then this basket of fruit; these are the best: the birds have pecked them. Our visitor is a connoisseur in such matters.

HARTWIG [*almost to himself*] Strange visitor who does not want to see anything!

GOTTHOLD [*suspiciously*] Hmm! but sees everything.

HARTWIG [*looking at him*] Ah! it's true; you too . . . —you . . .

GOTTHOLD [*humming*] Red beard and black hair/So beware; it's your affair.

MIKLAUS [*looking at him*] You and Hartwig both seem delighted by this departure?

GOTTHOLD [*indifferently*] Just a man who moves on.

HARTWIG [*grumbling*] A sallow man, a dangerous man!

GOTTHOLD [*in a low voice*] This one here is as pale as money! he is the colour of Judas.

HARTWIG [*after a pause to* GOTTHOLD] Such a fox can't have good fur,—as we students at Heidelberg used to say.

[*All three sit down around the fire now burning brightly.*]

MIKLAUS However, the young master seems to like his company. —Isn't he a kinsman? The late count of Auersperg presented him to the king once . . .

GOTTHOLD [*poking the fire*] Yes, the father rescued him from obscurity, and twenty years passed before the obligated fellow worried about the child.—There had to be this matter of inheritance, of pecuniary interest, before he recalled over there at the Prussian court that his cousin Count Axel of Auersperg, German prince—and, moreover, head of the oldest branch, was living alone with three old retainers, in a dilapidated fortified castle, buried in the midst of the immense Black Forest. Then, how he could find guides! and sleep in thatched cottages!—and ride horseback, endless days, through rough road, new clearings, steep passes!

HARTWIG [*worried*] Yes, you are right, Gotthold; this man is not a friend. I shall always remember the day he arrived last week;—wasn't it the eve of Palm Sunday?—After having crossed the deserted halls of the castle in Herr Zacharias' company, when he suddenly found himself—him, all bedecked with orders and crosses—in front of the young count—well, instead of extending both hands, he was struck silent for a moment!—We three, big greybeards, rusted cuirasses, veterans of old wars, today retainers devoted to exile, but who, I think, have each won our Iron Cross a little less easily than he his broad ribbons (meaning no offence),—he did not even acknowledge our presence.

GOTTHOLD [*thoughtfully*] The count in the mourning which goes so well with his powerful frame, rising and welcoming him with his grave simplicity, seemed like a young lion who bears his race in his eyes. I was proud of him, I was! as proud as the day when I had the honour of putting a foil in his fist for the first time.—And I go so far as to think that today my lord is, beyond any doubt, one of the most dangerous swordsmen in Germany, if not the most redoubtable.

HARTWIG [*raising his head and smiling*] Remember, in the presence of that traveller, Ukko could not have been a better courtier.—The fiendish innocent! Do you remember that he was holding in leash three ferocious greyhounds,—who were growling at the sight of the stranger,—and that he was smiling and bowing? And that he asked the master in an undertone if he should loose them on this unexpected relative?

GOTTHOLD Ha! ha! the rascal!

HARTWIG That page is worthy of the good old days. He brings gaiety to this old fortress, and what's more his mind is already decisive, subtle, and astonishing.—He's like a spark that does not flicker out!

GCTTHOLD And he is as nimble as a shadow!

MIKLAUS [*with an old man's pout*] He's a bad little charmer who plays too many tricks on me.

GOTTHOLD [*smiling*] Good old Miklaus! . . . Go on with you, let's warm our last dreamings in his beautiful youth, as we warm our three white beards in this good bright fire. Let him play,—even at our expense; his roguish smile revives us, and his company is good for us.

45

MIKLAUS All right, all right, so be it!

[*He stirs the fire.*]

—But to come back to our wolves,* you both surprise me when you would have me believe that our lord has no great liking for his cousin. Why from the very first meal the antique silver hollowware was brought out and the best corners of the cellar ransacked.

GOTTHOLD What does that prove? The count fills his duties as a host, that is all.

MIKLAUS However, Herr Zacharias . . .

HARTWIG As a matter of fact, what *does* the old steward say about it? He's a ferret;—a financier worthy of those times when each great lord had his goldsmith. I don't imagine that Commander Kaspar imposed upon *him* in the accounts of inheritance.

MIKLAUS On the contrary! Herr Zacharias has a very high and favourable opinion of him!

HARTWIG [*stunned, to* GOTTHOLD] Do you suppose old age has finally dulled his wits?

GOTTHOLD [*thoughtfully*] What Miklaus says does not surprise me. I have noticed that since the coming of our personage, Herr Zacharias is worried, silent . . . I don't know . . . he prowls around;—he is uneasy.

HARTWIG He has something on his mind.

GOTTHOLD [*in a lower voice*] And then he knows the time-honoured secrets of the family . . . , without counting . . . the DREADFUL one.

MIKLAUS and HARTWIG [*together*] Shush, Gotthold!

[*The three old men look around them anxiously as if fearing a mysterious eavesdropper.* GOTTHOLD *trembles and kicks the reddening logs vehemently with his heavy nailed boot. The logs suddenly burst into vast flames and shower sparks into the hall.*]

MIKLAUS [*resuming the conversation after a pause*] To conclude, *I* think Count Axel is in no way bored with his guest.—How

---

* Miklaus is playing on the cliché " revenons à nos moutons " (sheep)— " To get back to the subject."

46

could he be? why, he drinks in a supper with him more wine than he used to drink in a dozen meals. I believe that he is even getting a taste for it—and I am glad of it!

GOTTHOLD [*raising his head*] Good old Miklaus, you ought to know the young master a little better.

HARTWIG He who is so temperate that he fasts for days at a time!

GOTTHOLD He who deprives himself of all the joys of his youth! who uses the best years of his life to keep vigil there in the tower, and for so many nights!—under the study lamps, poring over old manuscripts in the company of the doctor.

HARTWIG [*to* MIKLAUS] Don't you understand that it is only because of court etiquette that he proposes toasts! The lord of the castle must do honour to his guest and give him his due.

MIKLAUS There, there!—Say what you please . . . *I* tell you that he has found distractions these past eight long days.—For example, these hunting parties with the Commander . . .

HARTWIG Don't count that! It's a way for him to be alone. Are you forgetting that he is fond only of silence!—If he sometimes accepts Ukko as a companion, it's because at his side the child becomes more silent than his shadow and because he knows that such a vigilant watchman with falcon eyes will love him until death!—With anyone else, with just a moment's gallop upon his stallion Wunder he is out of sight, crossing ravines and hedges. Gunter and Job, his two least aged huntsmen, gave up following him a long time ago,—Commander Auersperg almost always returns to the castle a half hour after leaving.

MIKLAUS [*musing*] Really? Ah? . . . that's different! I thought his cousin was helping him a little these past days in the dangerous battues in the underbrush.

HARTWIG [*smiling*] Axel of Auersperg has no need to summon anyone when he wants to destroy boars, bears, or eagles.

[*Pointing to the walls.*]

Look up there.—At the dangers! . . . By Saint Wilhelm! You know good and well that our young lord is so vigorous that he strangles wolves with a single grip at the throat without deigning to draw out his hunting knife.

[*In a lower tone of voice.*]

As for anything threatening him from afar, twenty thousand foresters of the Black Forest, miners, cobblers, woodcutters, old soldiers, all are more loyal to him than to the king!

MIKLAUS [*reflectively*] In fact—in fact, you could be right!—Besides, it is rather surprising that, as far as I know, he has not even asked Master Janus to leave his work and solitude for a minute to come examine the visitor a little.

GOTTHOLD [*after a pause*] Oh! the doctor knows people just by having them seen.

MIKLAUS [*looking at him*] Eh?

GOTTHOLD He perceives them, he divines them by the tone of voice of those who speak to him about them.

HARTWIG [*putting his hand on* GOTTHOLD'S *shoulder, laughing*] Come now!—Master Janus all the same is not a sorcerer, is he, Gotthold?

GOTTHOLD [*gravely*] I know what I'm saying. If the doctor has not once appeared, it's because the Commander is unimportant, scarcely worth a glance and in the end of no account.

[*A pause.*]

By the way . . . Have you noticed, Hartwig, that Master Janus does not grow old?—Yet he's been here many years!

HARTWIG Yes, that's true!

[*Laughing.*]

Apparently the cult of the stars prevents old age.

[*A pause. Only the crackling fire can be heard in the lofty hall.*]

GOTTHOLD [*perplexed*] To me his eyes do not seem to belong to a man of this century.

HARTWIG [*with a forced laugh*] Good old Gotthold wants to frighten us now.

MIKLAUS [*lowering his voice and speaking confidentially*] I admit that there is something in Master Janus which holds back affection. His manner of doing good works chills his debtors.—Gotthold, he has often healed us, and the peasants on the outskirts of the Great Forest; that makes no difference.

You never feel comfortable around him! For nearly a dozen years now I have waited on him daily. It's strange . . . but I cannot get used to it—even to believing that he sees me.

HARTWIG [*musing, also in an undertone*] Have we ourselves ever looked at him carefully? When he appears, he startles us like a stranger. When he speaks, a rare event, what he says, although always simple, seems like a reflection between two mirrors: you get infinitely lost in it. Listen! it's better not to think too much about the doctor,—if we have a care to keep our wits about us until we die.

GOTTHOLD [*gravely, in the same tone*] He is naturally unfathomable. The impression he makes on the mind even resists all the jostling of daily life.—When he arrived on horseback alone the very day of the unforeseen death of Court Gherard of Auersperg at the close of the wars against the mysterious Napoleon,—it was dawn. When they showed him the will and testament by which the count (who had, it appears, known Master Janus on the fields of battle) left to him the charge of rearing his son,—I was watching him. He acted as if he already knew about both the death and the last wish.

[*In a short time the sky outside has become overcast, and squalls announce an approaching tempest. Five o'clock strikes.*]

HARTWIG Listen: this is the hour when our beautiful, venerated chatelaine Lisvia of Auersperg, like the chatelaines of former times, used to go down to the chapel organ twenty years ago. She was always pensive and serious!

GOTTHOLD [*to* MIKLAUS] You know, don't you, the casement of the large gallery where the sunlight fades away in the evening? She used to linger there, often for long hours at a time—leaning on the sill, grown pale in her mourning, her expression like an angel's, and upon her knees her Book of Hours with enamel clasps.

MIKLAUS, GOTTHOLD, and HARTWIG [*rising and uncovering their heads*] May God be with the souls of the dead of this house!

[*They sit down again. A pause ; the beating rain is heard outside.*]

HARTWIG Come on, throw some pine cones on the front of the

hearth and let's have done with memories. The years are puffs
of wind, and we are the leaves they carry away.

GOTTHOLD Nevertheless, when Axel of Auersperg breaks his
silence on some solemn moment, in my opinion, this place will
ring.

MIKLAUS [*shaking his head*] The main doors bang in the strong
winds!

GOTTHOLD [*almost to himself*] Ah! the fact is that by nature he is
always becoming a man . . . a superman.

[*Peals of thunder; lights of a storm; distant echoes from the
woods.*]

MIKLAUS [*rising and going to a window*] But,—what weather! . . .
The sky has changed during our reminiscing! The storm torments the mountain. Fortunately, the keep is still solid.

GOTTHOLD [*standing, peering into the distance also*] That's true.
Already the flashes streak blue across the horizon. Look at the
pines, would you; how the thunderbolts light up the depths.

[*They listen to the storm.*]

HARTWIG And you can hear the creaking boughs from here. What
a downpour! Fortunately, the cannons between the crenellations
are covered and well oiled.

MIKLAUS How the gusts beat our old casements! It's doubling in
force. There will be no moon tonight. Accursed weather!
Probably the Commander will not be able to bring himself to
leave today.

GOTTHOLD [*tense*] Torrents of rain stream through the underbush.
With our lord still not back from the hunt!—Let's hope he
wore his leather jerkin!

[*A vast blue-violet flash furrows the shadows of the room.*]

MIKLAUS Ah! the thunderclap is going to burst!

GOTTHOLD It *was* a gloomy, hideous flash.

MIKLAUS I thought I caught a glimpse of hell!

HARTWIG [*after the clap*] And it's Easter Eve!

SCENE 3

[*The same, Ukko.*]

[*Ukko enters out of breath from the left. He has a hunting horn on his shoulder and a spike in his hand. He wears a black woollen sagum held by an iron-ringed leather belt; his fur bonnet has two eagle plumes.*]

UKKO Good evening, ancestors!

[*He puts his boar-spear in a corner and comes front.*]

GOTTHOLD, MIKLAUS and HARTWIG [*turning round*] Ukko!

UKKO [*gaily*] Were you three all pondering the admirable order of the seasons?

GOTTHOLD You left the hunt?—Where did you leave our lord?

UKKO In a cavern three miles from here—watching the storm come up.

HARTWIG And what kind of day was it?

UKKO A large lynx, a she-wolf and her litter, two foxes, and a vulture. The vulture was lost in black clouds, in thunder when the master's bullet took it by surprise. I killed the two foxes. But . . . there's another matter . . . and I want . . . .

MIKLAUS Drink this glass of Rhine wine and come warm yourself, ugly gnome.

UKKO [*drinking*] Thank you. I'm not cold.—I must tell you . . .

HARTWIG [*feeling his sleeve*] What! nothing underneath? He forgot his surcoat! . . . He is wet as grass.

UKKO It's nothing.—You should know . . .

MIKLAUS Come on, sit here ; or you will be sick ; warm yourself.

UKKO Come on, don't bother, I tell you!—Imagine . . .

HARTWIG [*worried*] Has something happened to the count?

UKKO No! Would I have left him?—Ah! if you knew . . .

MIKLAUS to GOTTHOLD The child has quite changed since yesterday in my opinion, what do you think? Did you realise you are quite pale, Ukko?

[UKKO *crosses his arms and watches them.*]

HARTWIG Speak quickly. You worry us.

UKKO [*stamping his foot impatiently*] By all the gods!

HARTWIG and MIKLAUS to GOTTHOLD [*who has been sitting silently *at the hearth*]   Be quiet, Gotthold. [*To* UKKO]   We're listening.

UKKO [*beginning his story*]   Yesterday evening . . .

MIKLAUS [*in an undertone*]   Listen, do you hear that thunder, eh?

UKKO [*furious*]   Ah!—You don't want to listen to me, do you?
. . . all right. I'm leaving—As garrulous centenarians, you have
no earthly peer!

GOTTHOLD   Silence! Let the child speak!

UKKO [*continuing*]   Imagine! You have nearly three centuries
between you,—you have heard thousands of storms, bolts of
lightning, north winds, and ghastly battles, and a mean little
squall interests you . . . when I have something I want to tell
you?

GOTTHOLD   There! there, madcap!

HARTWIG   Careful!

UKKO [*in the same tone of voice*]   But *I* am seventeen and seventeen only, and I am no more worried than that [*snaps his
fingers*] about wind, rain and all earthquakes.

MIKLAUS   Fine. Tell us what comes next . . .

UKKO   No. I prefer to leave. You will learn nothing from me. So
there.

GOTTHOLD   Will you please speak now, you imp? What's going
on?

UKKO   Miklaus and Hartwig will still interrupt me and then . . .
Besides, no: you don't like me . . .

HARTWIG [*smiling*]   Mischievous rogue!

UKKO   You are not interested in what happened to me.

MIKLAUS   Calm down and tell us . . .

UKKO   Good-bye.

[UKKO *takes a few steps as if to leave; the three old men throw
themselves upon him and bring him back, half smiling, half vexed.*]
[*Then, standing by the table flowers, lighted by the candelabra and
also by the flickers from the fireplace and the rare violet flashes,
he is a gleaming silhouette. He meditates while the three retainers,
seated around him, listen, vaguely anxious.*]
[*He speaks, smiling, as if lost in a dream—while from the depths
of the storm distant harps seem to accompany him.*]

   In the forest yesterday at the first star I met a little fairy, oh!

a thousand times prettier than all those in the Harz! . . . a girl. She was singing, and her voice was as fresh as the murmur of mountain streams. She balanced a little basket of wild cherries in one hand as she walked beneath the fir trees. Her two brown braids were knotted at the waist of her velours corselet with cowslips. From time to time she patted her big white spaniel who frisked gaily around her! Oh! she was so pretty!—Her eyes were as gentle as evening!

MIKLAUS [*smiling*] Ah! Ah! already young Ukko . . .

[GOTTHOLD *puts his hand over* MIKLAUS' *mouth*.]

For a while, hidden alongside her, I followed her in the glade. Suddenly I separated the brambles and went to her. Before our glances really met, we exchanged a friendly smile. However, we had never seen each other. We held out our hands to each other without a second thought. Her white companion looked at me intently ; he seemed to recognise me too ; a minute later he and my big greyhound, Holf, were old friends. Silently she and I in single file followed the path leading to the torrent where the oaks begin. There is the little cottage of her father, Hans Glück, the ranger. I entered. He looked up. Then having studied us carefully, he offered me his hand and welcomed me to his home. Luisa put two glasses on the white tablecloth. Ah! that good clear kirsch that she knows how to make so well! With her dear hands she poured for us during our chat . . . Since night had fallen by now, as she said good-bye to me on the threshold, I placed on her finger the family ring I hold dear.—Silent, she kissed me on the forehead ; her eyes were serious, and two beautiful tears fell from her lashes to my eyelids.—I fled! I was so happy that I began to weep as I went through the woods! I was gasping! Holf was barking and gleefully pulling me back to the little cottage.—Ah! Luisa Glück! It is from heaven— and from the pure fire of passion of her kiss—that I get this delightful desire for her in my soul! I cannot breathe! I am too full of love, too much in love—We shall marry in the autumn, at the latest!—I am . . . I am happy!—Only if one of you three should dare die before the wedding,—ah! . . . I shall be angry!

GOTTHOLD I shall be your best man, Ukko.

UKKO [*laughing and tweaking* GOTTHOLD'S *long beard*] Thank you, a million and one times.

[*He points to* MIKLAUS *and* HARTWIG] Here are some godfathers . .

HARTWIG How's this!—why I remember when she was born . . . your little Luisa, the day before yesterday!

UKKO [*musing, looking at him*] The day before yesterday?—Of course, that's right. For ordinary people that makes sixteen and a half years.

HARTWIG [*in an undertone*] Already!

UKKO One says "Already!" and the other "finally!" I am beginning to believe that it is the same word turned around.*

MIKLAUS [*laughing*] I find it strange that old man Glück—a brave Saxon soldier, to be sure—gives you his daughter, my friend.

UKKO [*putting a hand on* MIKLAUS' *shoulder*] You really are fortunate still to find things strange at your age.

HARTWIG Miklaus is not wrong this time ; you are good-looking, but you are a shadow.

UKKO My good Hartwig, don't you suffer from the shadow of your left arm when the weather changes?

HARTWIG Yes.—Why do you ask that, son?

UKKO [*joking*] Ah! ask *that* of the cannon ball which took away its reality at Lutzen. I just wanted to make you realise that a shadow *is* something.

GOTTHOLD The child is quite right to be happy, and as soon as possible. You are gloomy souls.—But, listen! I hear . . . eh? Those steps . . .

MIKLAUS Yes, in the Knights' Gallery.

HARTWIG It's our guest, I think.—Quick, some more logs on the fire, Miklaus!

UKKO Well, since I cannot possibly look both respectful and joyful when I see him, let's bow and leave.

GOTTHOLD That's who it is, all right.

UKKO [*bringing the three together, confidentially*] Listen— the future grandfather of your godsons gave me a jar of rose kirsch

---

* An author's slip; no one has used "finally" since Ukko has been on stage.

more precious than the king's. My friends, I invite you to come taste a bit of it in the armoury. There we shall feel at home. And while waiting for our master, our good Axel, gentleman of the woods, prince of the mountain, and lord of the torrents,—oh! I want you to drink with me to my fiancée, Luisa Glück!

MIKLAUS, GOTTHOLD, HARTWIG [*a finger on their lips*]   Shush!

[KASPAR OF AUERSPERG *enters from the right.—Very tall, he has the bearing of a very great lord. He is about forty-three. He wears an elegant travelling costume of black wool with a short cape. Upon his chest he wears the insignias of several orders.*]

SCENE 4

[*The same,* COMMANDER KASPAR OF AUERSPERG.]

COMMANDER [*to himself while studying them*]   No. Not these men. They are rocks,—and the child is the damned soul of his master.—The other one, the major-domo, * that Herr Zacharias, he is the one to attack.

UKKO   If the commander would like to wait for my lord here, he has Cape wine, tobacco, a warm fire, and books.

COMMANDER   The count is to return soon?

UKKO   In an hour at the latest.

[UKKO *and the three old soldiers bow and leave.*]

[*For the past few minutes the storm seems to have abated; it now thunders only at long intervals, and in the distance the rain has nearly stopped; through the windowpanes the sky remains overcast and threatening.*]

SCENE 5

[COMMANDER AUERSPERG *alone.*]

COMMANDER   Those are magnificent old men!—They bring to mind a beautiful battlefield, a beautiful winter, and a beautiful death.

---

* The Commander's error; Herr Zacharias is not the major-domo.

55

[*He looks around.*]

What an owls' nest!—Books, he says. Ancient history, no doubt? Let's see.

[*He open a folio.*]

The wine, let's postpone it; it is almost as old as those who bottled it. However, its marvellous vintage grows old without deteriorating.

[*He reads.*]

Treatise on Secondary Causes.

[*He laughs.*]

Ha! ah! excellent title! . . . *Treatise on Secondary Causes !* There is lucid jargon for you! . . . Ah! ah!—Let's read on a bit.

[*He resumes reading.*]

*Procul à delubro mulier semper !** That epigraph, one must admit, is not the last word in gallantry.

[*He continues.*]

Chapter I: *Silentiaries.*—What the devil! "Any word in the circumference of its action, creates what it expresses. Therefore, consider how much volition you grant to the inventions of your mind."

[*Closing the book, he throws it down upon the others.*]

Nonsense.

[*He yawns.—Then he muses after glancing at the objects around him.*]

It has already happened; I don't doubt it any longer—my young squire is becoming a prey to Hermeticism, Kabbalism, and the rigamaroles of the Black Mass. It must be this Master Janus who is breathing these notions in his head, instilling in him these befuddling superstitions . . . which will be the vice of Germany for a long time to come. Their conversations, I suppose, must take up the Holy Vehmegericht and the Rosicrucians. In fact, there were some of them in our family, but . . . when it was fashionable.—I can certainly understand why this gloomy madman has not judged it advantageous up to now to

---

* Let the woman keep away from the shrine forever !

expose himself to my profane eyes. I would have executed him handsomely with two or three thrusts.

[*A pause. He sits down at the table and pours himself a drink.*]

I have to admit, this manor, its inhabitants included, seems improbable, when I think of it. Here I find that *I* am a paradox. Here, they're three centuries behind, by the clock. Did I think that I was living in the dawn of the nineteenth century? I was wrong! . . . In crossing this threshold I perceived that I was living under Emperor Heinrich at the time of the Investiture Wars.

So be it.—To the health of said Emperor!

[*He drinks.*]

Now, all the same, I should really like to see clearly into this abnormal existence they lead in this household. As for my noble cousin, I feel only a somewhat moderate sympathy for this young hero of another age. He is truly a most elusive character. Moreover, any man at the approach of forty taking an interest in others besides himself is not worthy of life.

[*A pause.*]

But, let's see: he's a gentleman in the best sense, I must admit, although he has a somewhat tragic manner. With his tall stature he has even a superb overall bearing and does not lack a kind of untamed distinction . . . which would make the best effect at court, where they are bewitched by novelty. I can see right now the queen's lady musicians the evening of his presentation, —the Princess of Sabelsberg, the Countess of Walstein,—ah! ah! Incendiary success at first sight! or I am strangely mistaken.—He knew how to welcome me with perfect courtesy and showed what a great lord he was by surrendering to me his part of the inheritance despite his lost fortune . . . I am sure that if well directed, Count Axel of Auersperg could win for me with the king certain influences . . . of a very appreciable usefulness ;—and that old incident of his father and the Treasury is almost forgotten now!

[*After a pause.*]

—Oh! my old ambition, up to now always disappointed.

[*He darkens as he looks around.*]

And ambition is a sorceress, too.

[*His glance rests upon the table.*]

Here is my farewell supper. A table pleasing to the eye!—These pretty wild flowers . . . all in the best taste and extremely good taste.

[*A pause.*]

Even the air one breathes here is singular! In this old dwelling a presentiment of the unknown oppresses me.—Let's see. I think I have acquired some ascendancy over my young cousin. This type of person has the susceptibility of a child, really.—I have a twenty-year advantage over him. This, joined to our blood ties, has allowed me a certain ease, which I have quickly turned to familiarity—acting protective in our talks. In short, an apparent carelessness of speech with well-calculated candour, if increased gradually, will be tolerated imperceptibly up to the point of impertinence . . . This evening I must try to combat the influence of this Master Janus. By the time we reach dessert I want to show him that his Great Task is to make his way in the world and to take there, one way or another, the places he desires to occupy.

[*Thoughtfully.*]

As if all the phantasmagorias on earth and all philosophers' opinions were worth as much in reality as a pretty woman's glance! And youth, alas! beautiful youth!—There is real magic!—A beautiful creature,—that is something everyone understands at once! effortlessly! That is what is clear!

[*He holds his crystal glass up against the candlelight.*]

I can readily imagine that all these sombre surroundings— woods, torrents, valleys—heightened by solitude, have nurtured these absurd ideas in his mind.—Bah! the sickness would cure itself in a week at the court . . . And I am sure that in my hands this young man would become a most useful instrument.

[*He rises and paces back and forth.*]

All the same, I am worried.—It is not natural that a boy, who certainly has no common mind, would deliberately accept the bearish existence that Count Axel of Auersperg leads here! All love whatsoever of occult science would not explain such a seclusion, such a long, remote, and voluntary exile.—There is something else.

[*He looks around the room silently. Then in a lower and singularly musing tone.*]

—Something here is responsible.

[*He reflects while watching distractedly the gleams of distant lightning.*]

Now I've spent eight long days in this forgotten, crenellated, obsolete lair where the architecture, surroundings, and silence could interest only vain ideologists. Now I certainly should not have been preoccupied at such length if I had not had a confused, tenacious intuition of some kind of mystery!—Since this feeling preoccupies me still, it means that it is well-founded and . . . I don't like to beat around the bush. I should like very much to clear up this enigma.—It would have been rather imprudent to question Herr Zacharias before now; but, since I am leaving this worrisome pile today, and without regrets, I can, in a little while, when the old steward . . .

[*Seeing Herr Zacharias enter.*]

Here he is.

SCENE 6

[COMMANDER KASPAR OF AUERSPERG, HERR ZACHARIAS.]

HERR ZACHARIAS [*on the threshold, looking at the Commander*]
The hour has come. It is my duty to speak.

[*He closes the door cautiously.*]

COMMANDER [*to himself, looking at the steward*] If he is a sorcerer, too, I must say that the devil takes his time carrying him off.

[*He studies him from head to foot.*]

Well now! but . . . that fellow must be a hundred years old! Let's study these remains a bit: opaque diplomatic eyes, thin lips . . . yes, but a nose that shows no shrewdness. Good.

[*Aloud.*]

Good evening, Herr Zacharias! Whatever is the matter?—I'd swear by my pillbox that you look upset.

HERR ZACHARIAS [*with serious mien, drawing near the Commander*]
My lord, I have more than once had the honour of meeting you,
some twenty years ago.—You were a friend of the late count;
you must be devoted to his son.

COMMANDER [*to himself*]   Devotion is his vulnerable side.
[*Aloud.*]
He is a young man with a future, and I should make every
sacrifice to see him assume his rank in the world.

HERR ZACHARIAS   My lord, I have pondered night and day since
your arrival. My remaining days of life are numbered; your
presence is an opportunity, completely unexpected, and I must
seize it.

COMMANDER   My presence?

HERR ZACHARIAS [*preoccupied*]   Yes, I have something fantastic I
want to disclose to you. Something . . . Oh! the strangest of
all things!—If you want to hear about it, I must hurry; it is
part of a complicated story . . . the hour passes and—you are
leaving tonight.

COMMANDER   You are too solemn to be serious, Herr Zacharias!

HERR ZACHARIAS   My lord, I never speak without weighing all my
words carefully. Now it is really impossible to find words exact
enough to describe the facts which I desire to present to you.
In short, if there is on this earth a secret meriting the title of
SUBLIME—certainly, we can say it is this one. Only to think
about it . . . gives me vertigo . . . You see: I am distracted . . .
just talking about it!

[*The tempest roars. He looks around.*]

COMMANDER [*after a moment*]   This secret, does it affect the count
and me?

HERR ZACHARIAS   First of all. Then Germany. Then . . . the whole
world.

COMMANDER [*to himself*]   This old man!—Hum! This unexpected
frankness bothers me.—How shall I react?—With indifference
or attention?—Indifference is preferable; he is going to have to
exert himself to convince me.
[*Aloud.*]
Speak.—But here you are as grave as an ambassador from the

60

Orient. You make me apprehensive.—Is your story very long?

HERR ZACHARIAS I believe that I have the means to assure you that you will have no regrets whatsoever if you listen until the end.—Within a half-hour the count undoubtedly will return. I have therefore just time enough to tell everything, and silence has oppressed me for—oh! for so many years!

[THE COMMANDER, *illuminated by the candlelight, smiles and pours himself a drink. He sits with his legs crossed, his elbows on the table.*]

[HERR ZACHARIAS, *stands in front of the fire; his hands rests on the back of the opposite chair. He lowers his voice a little.*]

Does not my lord remember an extraordinary event which took place in Germany—and which had world-wide repercussions,—at the time of the death of Count Gherard of Auersperg?

COMMANDER [*smiling*] An extraordinary event?

HERR ZACHARIAS Yes.

COMMANDER I have never seen anything extraordinary under the sun, Herr Zacharias!—Except . . .

[*Suddenly as if struck by a dim memory, he trembles, looks fixedly at the old steward and remains speechless a moment.—Then in a grave, altered voice.*]

Go ahead.*

[*At this command Herr Zacharias pulls from his greatcoat a military map and divers papers which he unfolds silently, then spreads out upon the table in front of Commander Auersperg.*]

---

* The Commander starts using " tu "

II

The Story of Herr Zacharias

HERR ZACHARIAS [*at first speaks in the tone of someone reciting a written discourse, long committed to memory,—then, little by little, he becomes animated and improvises.*] Here are the papers and documents ; they have bearing on the precise moment of our history when the event of which I speak took place. At that time we were under the brunt of that invasion which today seems to us like some disastrous daydream.

At the news of each successive defeat suffered by our armies in central Germany, there soon were some semi-official rumours that the enemy was preparing a sudden offensive to the rear against the various states situated behind its apparent line of march. Immediately the cities of the zone which thought it was threatened—(The electoral and financial free-city of Frankfort in particular)—began to tremble in advance at the exactions and violence that the French soldiery would be sure to inflict.— Recruiting, especially, was marked by so many harsh acts over in the invaded provinces!—Napoleon seemed to rise up on all sides at once.—Because with that strange captain who in three days was suddenly thirty leagues from where our calculations supposed him to be, we had to expect grim surprises. It was a time of panic ; they didn't believe there even was time to use the war loan which had just been raised. Remember, my lord, how those cities of the interior used to look, those closed houses, that mourning, that distant fusillade, and that perpetual cannon noise,—the tocsin dispersed by the wind on all the roads . . .

COMMANDER Let's skip over that part.

HERR ZACHARIAS However, even in those states which were so alarmed, they were ignorant of the real extent of the peril, for at that precise moment a financial circumstance of the most unheard of variety had trebled the calamity. In effect, for nearly

63

five weeks before those foreboding rumours, gold coin had come flowing in from all districts, as a result both of a sort of panic and a rush of confidence, both irrational—(these phenomena are not at all rare in wartime). This coin had been flowing into the vaults of the National Bank of Frankfort.

[*He unfolds an old, yellow-looking paper.*]

Vainly, in order to try to stem the tide the Bank had given notice that its holdings no longer permitted it to accept anything more except gold specie. Here is the detailed inventory of the securities that were there then,—securely stored to be ready if needed under the low vaults of the great Treasury,—in . . . nearly four hundred iron strongboxes, sealed with the insignia of the Confederation:

Assets, gold coin of the public reserve, backed by fiduciary paper, suspended from circulation by the sudden interruption of normal business and negotiation in Germany: 42 million thalers.—Assets coming from the recent issue of the war loan: 76 million thalers ; all legal tender.—Sacks of deposits of valuables committed to the custodian city, cut diamonds, jewels of great price, divers gems collected in necklaces and falls, fine pearls, gold plate, art mountings, pure gold bars and ingots, total estimated value, 78 million thalers.—Consignments in gold specie from private banks in Wurtemberg, Bavaria, Saxony, and the Grand Duchies on account as sums placed without interest in the safeguard of the surety of the State, 75 million thalers—Divers deposits from the upper classes, both nobility and bourgeoisie, 26 million thalers, all in gold currency.—Etc., etc.—Total of cash reserve thus stored in the subterranean shelters and subsidary vaults of the Treasury: around 350 million thalers: this being in round figures the unbelievable, immeasurable negotiable assets of more than eleven hundred million French francs, representing the suddenly suspended circulation of more than two-thirds of the gold coin, both foreign and German mintage.

COMMANDER [*preoccupied, observing him carefully*] Yes, I know. Go on.

HERR ZACHARIAS That is why since the news of an offensive

toward that point in Germany was decisively accredited, the High Commission of Finance of the Confederation came to address the regents of the Treasury the following memorandum: " Whereas a considerable percentage of these securities has been officially designated for military use, the imperial conqueror could in all legality,—under pretext of a preventive and defensive war measure,—sequester the whole of these enormous liquid assets. Whereas all subsequent efforts at recovery being likely to present difficulty or litigation, whatever be the issue of the campaign,—there is cause, following the precedent in these exceptional circumstances, to take at this very instant urgent dispositions to direct these securities without delay to a part of the territory far from the action of the belligerents—and situated, as far as is possible, beyond the conceivable attacks of the enemy ".—Therefore, on the receipt of this decree the Financial Council of the National Bank, having met in secret session, chose for the direction of that grave and perilous undertaking three of the most highly esteemed of the general officers on duty at military posts near the city. These were the General Prince of Muthwild, the General Count of Thungern, and finally the General Count Gherard of Auersperg who accepted the command.

[*A pause.*]

COMMANDER [*thoughtfully, to himself*] Yes, it is a fact in German history which has remained a positive enigma.

HERR ZACHARIAS In his estimation two thousand Saxon cavalrymen and eighty artillery wagons would be sufficient. Different orders to forestall all immediate enemy attacks were addressed at once to the commanders of surrounding divisions. They were going to set off towards the quarter-southwest; they would follow unfrequented roads,—the Count of Auersperg at the head of the detachment, the Count of Thungern in the center, and the Prince of Muthwild in the rear guard,—and by a wide circuit they would reach the fortified city known only to them.

The very evening of that decision the four hundred precious iron strongboxes under the collective label of cannon, war munitions, and heavy projectiles, were hoisted, loaded, then bound fast by chains and ropes upon eighty munition wagons, all this in the principal courtyard of the Bank.

—Upon higher orders, the courtyard was deserted by all regular employees. It was encircled during the operation by the escort squadrons, defiling in front of the main entrance and receiving two convoy wagons per fifty horsemen.

At midnight they left the city, plunged in total darkness, its street lights extinguished.

—Towards what citadel, agreed upon among the three commandants and the Treasury regents, were they going first? . . . No doubt this was revealed in high places later.—The fact remains that on the basis of repeated warnings from the scouts, after two days of march toward the most central southwest, Count Auersperg, perhaps having grounds for fearing a strange accident to his vanguard, changed the itinerary hastily on his own initiative in the name of the frightening responsibility which weighed on his military honour. And, no longer trusting anyone, he perhaps intended to inform those who had a right to know only after the *essential* accomplishment of the heavy task he had accepted.

COMMANDER [*pale and smiling*] Sit down Zacharias. This recitation is wearing out your voice. Drink a bit of this wine— glittering and red like all that gold you are talking about!— This will revive you.

HERR ZACHARIAS [*refusing with a gesture, bows, and seems little by little to lose himself in a visionary dream.*] Undoubtedly, then—at the back of his mind rose the image of an impenetrable fortress, lost amidst calm and terrible forests, a hundred leagues long, and with paths, familiar from his childhood, which appeared to him practicable for those narrow wagons following after him with a part of the fortune of Germany!

—Undoubtedly he remembered also there in those same forests an inviolable receptacle, excavated for centuries.—A site of tenebrae, with accesses known to him alone, could, at least until the imminent peace, keep—faithfully!—what was entrusted to its deep entrails. Therefore, it was towards this

66

site that he decided to guide—by routes totally removed from any possible hostile encounter—the men and the treasure for which he was answerable to the fatherland . . . And this, my lord,—mark well! *into this forsaken region where we are.*

[*The* COMMANDER *starts and looks at him in great stupefaction.*]

Most certainly, beneath the interminable forest surrounding this fortress, beneath some massive rock covered today by trees and undergrowth, must be hidden the entrance to one of those subterranean tunnels excavated since before the middle ages,—with secrets known only by the elders of the high military seigneury to whom the tunnels belonged,—and which, formerly, served for revictualing the fortress and for nocturnal sorties in case of blockade . . . And, remembering effortlessly the way to that unforgettable entrance—which, in his mountainous sections of the Great Forest must open to the interior on a steep incline . . .

COMMANDER [*interrupting him*] Here I can no longer listen to you.—If we can, in effect, suppose that Count Auersperg in this fantastic resolution which you impute to him may have thought himself able to hide on his own territorial domains these important " wartime munitions " without awaking suspicion, how can we believe that he would have dared put himself at the mercy of the discretion of two thousand men who the next day would surely talk over, among themselves at first, their singular task the night before? Even if we admit that the thought might have momentarily occurred to him—disturbed as he was by so many grievous alarms,—how can we believe that commanding officers such as the Prince of Muthwild and the Count of Thungern would not have dissuaded him, refusing their concurrence?—You are dreaming, Zacharias.

HERR ZACHARIAS [*as if lost in his thoughts, as if not even hearing the interruption*] Yes, it must have been through some rainy twilight, darkened further by the thick foliage and dense thickets, that he was leading, through the wide Forest footpaths,—to within some hundred steps from the precise spot where this lair, still out of sight, would respond to the knock of the hereditary master and open wide—yes,—that he was leading . . .

[*Raising his head and regarding the* COMMANDER *fixedly.*]

A simple detachment, oh! some two hundred men, perhaps! —just the few necessary from the wagon convoy!—having left behind the rest of his escort, useless from now on, one or two leagues from the outskirts of the forest.—Once he had reached this uninhabited country, isolated for all time, he had crossed the circle of dangers.

[*As if having an hallucination.*]

At the sudden cry of halt from the Count of Auersperg, the winding column of wagons and horsemen is stopped, and the Count of Thungern, leaving the center division, comes to station himself in front of the first convoy. Auersperg, having dismounted, has advanced alone and rather far off, reconnoitering his lines of trees,—and, at the turning of some ancient hedge of interlaced branches and high green underbrush, he has suddenly disappeared.—No one around him.—Advancing among fallen shadows, he considers certain rocks veiled by moss and grass, which his first glance has distinguished from other grey stones in their midst.—He has stretched full-length among their crevices, according to the secret transmitted to him by his father who had it from his father one day when *they* were alone. And with a special pressure, he makes the powerful, rusty levers of olden times creak underground, and here are two of these enormous rocks separating, forcing open the entrance, centuries old. Then straightening up, he summons each of the wagons to him, rapidly one after another, defiling in turn before the gaping aperture.

In the dim light of big lanterns, quickly lighted, three men from each wagon used to cannon manoeuvres have automatically fastened to the back of their vehicles an iron inclined plane upon which (since the cables were cut loose by axes) the metal strongbox casks, laterally maintained by side-guards of the inclined plane, can glide. They roll precipitously down the subterranean slope, and, sped along by their own momentum, plunge violently into the boundless depths of the long cavern. And the wagon moves away, continuing the forest path, soon joined by the next wagon,—and so on until the very last.

Two hours have sufficed. The two other leaders have silently resumed their places at the extremities of the detachment, where the Count of Auersperg will come rejoin them at a pre-arranged spot. He has stayed behind alone in the black night and soon he has made the earth-covered mobile rocks, which had separated or risen, fall again over the forbidden entrance. And it is over! The intoxicating treasure is thoroughly buried in impenetrable tenebrae.

Now, my lord, being given, first the deep-seated and quite natural impression that the four hundred iron casks contained as is usual in the artillery only magazines of lead, powder, or steel,—only some common war munitions, in effect—(besides, considering the number of casks, how could the truth be imagined!)—the men of this special detachment, chosen among those coming from the Saxon territories the furthest from the Black Forest,—purposely led astray in the woods, through a thousand twisting paths where only the Count of Auersperg could know where he was,—wearied by the long manoeuvres, worried about an encounter with the enemy in the environs of an imaginary fortress where they thought they were revictualing casemates,—their eyes blindfolded, so to speak, with their sudden arrival in the rain at nightfall and, with their retreat, by night,—rejoined soon by the count himself in the course of their perilous march,—and to be moved forward the next day to distant points in the thick of military action—how could this or that suspicion which one or the other of them might have had not have been completely ineffectual? And besides, since peace was said to be in the offing, what plundering could be feared from then on?

COMMANDER [*very calmly, watching Herr Zacharias*] What an ingenious story you have concocted, my dear Zacharias! . . . History, alas! is quite different. It tells us that the three commanding officers of whom you speak had been officially charged by the Upper Council of Finance of the Confederation to transport some immense national reserve to a citadel in west Germany. Compelled to unforeseen detours by the flanking maneouvres of French troops, the convoy had to go along the Bavarian frontier,—then advance towards the interior: doing this according to the march indicated on the maneouvre maps.

HERR ZACHARIAS On the one right in front of you.

COMMANDER Now this was more than twenty-five leagues from any approach to the Black Forest, where—as a result, it is true, of a circumstance still unexplained—General Auersperg as well as his two lieutenants were found together one day somewhat in advance of the convoy,—which, without any doubt, was captured by the enemy. They were seen by a reconnaissance brigade of French sharpshooters from a high observation post . . .

HERR ZACHARIAS [*placing a finger on the map*] Here is the precise spot!

COMMANDER Since from the ridge the enemy could not take them prisoner, it opened fire on them, stiff, continuous, brutal fire which left no man alive, apparently, exterminating them in less than a quarter hour. The Count of Auersperg was found with bullet holes in his head and chest; and that was pretty much the fate of his two seconds.—Confronted by this more than equivocal tragedy, I can only agree with consensus that this wartime incident, together with the ruinous capture or inconceivable disappearance of colossal riches . . . dispersed somehow . . . will always be one of the most extraordinary enigmas of History.

HERR ZACHARIAS My lord, I have confirmed to my satisfaction that a premeditated perfidy, an act of treachery, with a delayed explosion for the high-placed who planned it, was hidden beneath the apparent " tragedy " of that military assassination.—Ah! how many times I have felt myself on their tracks in the course of the extensive investigation which I have so patiently worked out! . . . What good is it even to reveal to you that the account book, counterfoil of the receipts delivered with the names of the depositors has been destroyed, burned! I have proof of it!—It is enough for you to know that the enemy captured only the munitions wagons, *still under cover, but empty!*—that Count Gherard of Auersperg before entering the Forest had sent into combat on the frontiers of the central principalities the rest of his two thousand men which he had only to rejoin,—the reverse of recorded History!—That accounts for the small number of cavalry around him during the fatal event which happened . . . exactly two days after the facts which I have just reconstructed.

COMMANDER [*after a moment*] What is your basis for considering them, facts?

HERR ZACHARIAS [*lowering his voice*] Two evenings before the very day he was to be killed, the Count of Auersperg came here, to the castle, around midnight.

COMMANDER [*going white, rising with a start*] You are sure of this?

HERR ZACHARIAS [*calmly*] I happened to be still up working in the lower hall of the keep when I heard first his horse galloping across the main postern,—and then suddenly I saw Count Gherard come in, hiding his uniform under a cavalry cloak.

COMMANDER Here? Him? . . . —Why?

HERR ZACHARIAS [*a little astonished*] Why, I suppose to embrace in tender farewell her who was to give him a son in a very few days! (He was supremely devoted.) Countess Lisvia of Auersperg, then pregnant with my Lord Axel, had taken refuge here during the war, and, weak and sickly, was always confined to her bed; thus she had at least the joy of seeing her husband again before death reunited them. The tragic news of the evening two days later was kept from her until the end.—Perhaps on this precipitous visit, so brief, the Count of Auersperg left some undiscovered written instructions destined for this son in the event that the perils, which he perhaps foresaw, would leave him an orphan. What became of this testament? Did it even exist? I do not know.

COMMANDER [*who has regained his composure and whose mind*

has wandered a moment] Herr Zacharias, in spite of myself, I somewhat question the reality of all that visionary speculation! But, sir, why have you told me such a secret?*

HERR ZACHARIAS Alas! because I am very old, my lord! and because I am going to die.—Because inaction in this case takes on the proportions of a crime,—and because I have not dared carry with me to the grave remorse for having kept silent! Because meaningless indemnities having been voted earlier, the receipts, thus redeemed by the states at a low rate, are actually abolished—and because in reality this prodigious treasure *now no longer belongs to anyone!* . . . Because my master to whom I have revealed everything, —with details which show my conjectures even better founded, —not only has never attempted or planned anything that I know of to recover this incalculable wealth, but has formally forbidden anyone to speak to him about it ever again! Because he made us, myself and three others, take an oath to make no further allusion to it, even among ourselves, even in a whisper.—Today, three years have passed since that oppressive oath . . . and never a word! I do not know what unheard of and terrible science Master Janus teaches him . . . but in truth it would seem . . . *that he has forgotten!* . . . No one in high places would listen to me, an old man buried in these remote forests!—You, my lord, are powerful. Kings listen to you! I therefore considered myself empowered to violate an oath, a criminal one anyway, in order that you might act in the name of my too indifferent master. Thus glory, power, and fortune will come to him in spite of himself! . . . And I wanted to acquit myself of this duty to the memory of his noble father, your kinsman and friend.

[*A horn is heard approaching from a distance.*]

Here is my Lord Axel!—Declare yourself now.

COMMANDER [*who has looked at him meaningfully*] Herr Zacharias, you are a wise and loyal servant. All that I can

---

* At this point the Commander resumes " vous ".

72

reply is that I leave tonight,—and that within three months you in this castle will hear from me.

[HERR ZACHARIAS *shows his pleasure.*]

THE COMMANDER [*to himself, reflecting*] That's what we say. My room is ready less than an hour's ride from here by the lower footpaths at the ostelry of the Three Storks,—at the crossroads of Wood-Cross; Otto, my valet, and the two first guides wait for me there . . . I can be there by eleven thirty this evening. Thus I shall be rested for the first six leagues of the way. Tomorrow, then, at dawn, away! And within a few days, out of the Forest! And . . . in post-chaise until Berlin! there, once I recoup my wrecked fortune, if I go about it prudently . . . why not attempt, alone and in secret, the conquest of this fantastic Golden Fleece? . . . O surprising revelation! . . . If only it is true!

[*Steps ring in the vestibule.*]

THE COMMANDER [*in a lower tone, a finger on his lips*] Silence.

[AXEL OF AUERSPERG *appears at the back of the room. He looks about twenty-three or twenty-four. He is very tall and has an admirable virile beauty. Both his robust elegance and the proportions of his frame indicate powerful physical strength. His face, almost radiantly pale, emerging from long, wavy brunette hair, has an expression rendered mysterious by its excessive pensiveness.*]

[*He is wearing a black leather suit with steel buttons. His otter bonnet has an eagle plume. He has a carabine at his shoulder, an axe at his belt.*]

[*For a moment he stands immobile on the threshold of the hall.*]

III

The Exterminator

[*The same,* AXEL OF AUERSPERG.]

AXEL Cousin, your humble servant.
COMMANDER Hello, Axel.—Did you have good hunting?*
AXEL [*smiling*] Always.
COMMANDER In this hell-sent weather? You *are* the *Black Huntsman!*—Do you hear that? . . . It sounds like demons thronging the avenue!
AXEL [*going to hang up his heavy carabine between two of the eagles on the wall*] In April bad weather clears quickly.—Do you still want to leave us this evening?
COMMANDER [*after catching* HERR ZACHARIAS' *eye*] I must; the king does not wait.
[*With that word* HERR ZACHARIAS, *delighted, leaves the room.*]
AXEL [*smiling*] Long live the king!
[*In a gracious, ceremonious voice.*]
    And . . . shall we sit down to dinner?
COMMANDER Excellent idea; I have an appetite.
[*They sit down.*]
[*The rain has stopped; the storm apparently has retreated to the woods.*]

SCENE 8

AXEL, *the* COMMANDER, UKKO, *then* GOTTHOLD, MIKLAUS, *and* HARTWIG.]

[UKKO, *followed by* HARTWIG, *enters from the rear; the latter holds a heavy wine basket in his only hand;*—GOTTHOLD *and* MIKLAUS, *coming from the right, carry silver vessels laden with*

---

* Axel uses "vous"; the Commander uses "tu".

dishes of food. UKKO *takes two of the dusty bottles and uncorks them.*]

COMMANDER [*to himself, thoughtfully*] It would seem *that he has forgotten!* . . . Herr Zacharias told me.—I must assure myself first on that point.

UKKO [*filling crystal hanaps half-full*] Burgundy.

AXEL [*unfolding his napkin*] So, you do not drink the *maytrank* with us. That's too bad; I think you would have found in it the fresh *parfum* of our springtime.

COMMANDER [*in the same carefree manner*] What can I do about it!—To your health.

[*He drinks, then studies the wild game which* GOTTHOLD *is carving.*]

Eh! a quarter of two-year-old wild boar!—I thought I took in its heady bouquet in the hall! But I wonder: would the scullion have left out the red pepper and vanilla in the cooking?

[*He tastes.*]

Not at all; it's perfect.

AXEL [*to* MIKLAUS] A little water, please.

COMMANDER [*laughing, in a very free and easy tone*] Speaking of boar, I had some excellent boar at the home of the aulic councillor Johannes Herner the day I received the chamberlain keys from his Majesty the King. The preparation, nevertheless, was different, if I remember correctly. Yes. That day the old male boar* had required French truffles, English spices, and Sicilian bay leaf. Festooned in clear quince jelly, it was served gleaming upon a bed of herbs.—Axel, I recommend the recipe to your head-cook; a gentleman cannot be too careful about his table.

AXEL Tell me, cousin: you turned back to the castle this afternoon; does hunting bore you?—or did you think you should conserve your strength for the two hundred leagues you are going to cover?

---

* The Commander uses the poetic "le solitaire", a term for a lone old male boar.

COMMANDER [*eating and drinking*]   I just wanted to sleep delight-
fully to the distant sounds of your tireless hunting horn.

AXEL [*in the same manner*]   And—did you have beautiful dreams?

[UKKO *silently pours for the two diners.*]

COMMANDER [*negligently, his intention hidden, almost
imperceptible*]   Golden dreams. I dreamt of that ancient
Lydian king who had only to throw a net into his Pactolian
river to draw out a netful of massive gold fish.—A beautiful
dream!

AXEL [*looking at him intently, and after a pause, raising his
gothic German glass*]   To its realisation!

COMMANDER [*to himself, undecided*]   Hmmm! . . .

[*He leans back smiling against the back of his chair. Aloud.*]

Axel, I am in a melancholy mood this evening,—and it is not
only because I'm leaving you.—To be sure, the table is
resplendent, the tablecloth and this old Bohemian crystal
are a beautiful sight! But . . . we are alone,—and, up there
at the court suppers beneath the candelabra, the glitter of
gold plate blends so beautifully with the women's white
complexions! Their eyes and their malicious little white teeth,
their smiles—so absurd and bewitching—blend so well with
the candlelight! Red flowers, especially red roses, go so nobly
with black hair! And even the silk, bathed in their perfumes,
everything in their presence adds the most unconquerable
magic to the delirium of a well-appointed supper! Ah! my
dear fellow, if you would just leave this exile and deign
to follow me into the world of merriment, luxury, and
love . . .

[*Lowering his voice a little and in a jovially fatuous tone.*]

—For example, suppose you saw, even just once, the lovely
Princess of Muthwild?

AXEL [*after an imperceptible shudder at the name*]   Well, what
would come of it, Commander?

COMMANDER [*to himself, undecided*]   Hmmm!

[*Aloud.*]

Why you would never sleep again! Think of it: a veritable
child, a widow, spiritual as can be for having waited with

77

downcast eyes for the death of her husband . . . with an angel's patience!—The dear prince! . . . According to one account, his father, an esteemed general, must have met the same fate as your noble father, killed in a surprise attack by a company of enemy sharpshooters during the invasion. The line is extinct.

[*A pause.*—AXEL *has listened impassively.*]

So that without having to remarry, Princess Karola at her Berlin palace can do as she pleases, protected from gossip by the mourning wreath on her coat of arms. And, I tell you, if once at her nocturnal feasts she let you—let *you,* the beloved sight unseen!—If she let you glimpse her sparkling blue eyes,—and her beautiful lips!—between the crystal of your glass and the flickering of the candles . . . you would lose sleep over it.

AXEL You think so?

COMMANDER [*laughing*] He doubts it! . . . Ah! do not slander yourself; do not reduce your future friends to idleness.

AXEL Are the women in society up there that fascinating?

COMMANDER For the most part. And then . . .

[*Speaking confidentially.*]

Remember, the giddiness that comes from ravishing them in front of their ever-present husbands—really trebles the joy of conquering them. After three society affairs hardly any man desires Properpine unless her savour is seasoned with the raving jealousy of sombre Pluto!—I read in your eyes the surprise which goes with your age;—but, for us, in many a gallant circumstance the poignant torture of the husband ardently in love sometimes constitutes the principal attraction of the wife who prefers us. This condiment, which all understand and which often decides us, seasons so well that amusement of elegant taste called love!

AXEL Really?—I thought there were still women of a more serious nature.

COMMANDER Come now, all women maintain a sovereign charity; only, they have their poor. That's what society calls virtue. —As for their sentiments . . .

[*He breathes deeply a small bouquet of forest flowers placed among his wine glasses.*]

What difference does it make if these flowers with so voluptuous a perfume have a grave heart or a frivolous one?

AXEL   You won't have anymore of this pheasant pâté, cousin?

COMMANDER [*accepting*]   Austere wolf-slayer, I want you to know that ordinary pâté seems the heaviest of metals,* but this one, conceived in inspiration, justifies the imprudence of my adventurous course!   [*A pause.*]

And you, Axel? You are eating little, I notice, and ... you look worried!

AXEL   I am thinking that the downpour must have hollowed ruts in the road. Ukko, you will unleash two of the mastiffs to beat down the high grass in front of us. You will saddle the horses about ten o'clock with a dark-lantern on the saddle-bows. I shall ride Wunder.

COMMANDER   By the way, what is that bizarre hour striking?

AXEL [*smiling*]   It is not a clock:—the tornado has swept into the tower, and is knocking the clapper against the alarm-bell, but it is nine o'clock, I suppose.

COMMANDER [*observing* AXEL]   Ha! ah! It is the hour when the merchant goes to sleep, "the conscience easy". Our good ancestors are no longer there to plunder a little on the roads. —Yes, once we used to lighten the merchants' load of loot from time to time, it is true! the "honest" bourgeois, the "honest" merchants, the "honest" Jews—the fine flower of human flora, you know!—And we robbed them without even inquiring by what thefts, usury, and ruses their honest savings were the entirely too legitimate fruit. In truth, I do not blame our forerunners' style too much! In all ages hasn't it been the right of the huntsman to tear the game from his dogs' jaws. —In reality, even the right by which lords justified themselves was not that of the strongest, but of the boldest!—They were one against a thousand; people obeyed them. Why? Because strength comes with courage, the sole touchstone of men of

---

* 'Métaux'. Apparently a slip of the commander who should have said 'mets' (courses).

79

race! I do not confuse honour and honesty.

AXEL [*as if he had not been listening*] Ukko and I shall accompany you as far as the crossroads of Wood-Cross because you could get lost in the outskirts or meet wolves.

MIKLAUS The carabines are ready, my lord, as well as the spears and hunting knives.

COMMANDER [*abruptly cold and sombre to himself, studying* AXEL] Come now, it is unimaginable! but our Herr Zacharias is right, I believe;—he's a carefree fellow who has forgotten.— Who knows! For my success I would have working for me darkness and the roar of the streams!—Night-time accidents in the Black Forest are natural enough. If I dare get it over with right away, a couple of shots,—would clear up the situation. Am I not the heir? And . . . of what an inheritance, perhaps!

AXEL *Where* is Walter Schwert?

GOTTHOLD My lord, he went to the village to replenish the castle provisions.

HARTWIG He will surely be soaking wet, and lynx, you know, prowl on bad nights . . .

MIKLAUS Oh! Franz is making the trip with the major-domo. They took with them their firearms, three of the fierce dogs, —and Rasch, the dog who does not bark . . .

AXEL Poor old man! [*To* MIKLAUS.] You will have some old French wine mulled for him.—Ah! . . . In the future I do not want him going out so late.

COMMANDER [*distractedly in an undertone, while putting his napkin on the table*] How you take care of them!

AXEL [*after a glance at the windowpanes*] But the sky has cleared; the stars are out.— Will you come again, cousin?

COMMANDER [*raising his eyes and looking at him*] Soon I hope.

AXEL To your forthcoming return!

[*They drink, then rise from the table.*]

COMMANDER [*smiling and with a sudden impulse of cordiality*] Axel, you* have a decidedly happy nature and—do give me your attention!

---

* The Commander resumes " vous ".

I have made up my mind to ask you a very special question
before I leave. I have something to say to you alone.

[*At a sign from the* COUNT OF AUERSPERG, MIKLAUS *and* GOTTHOLD
*have carried the table with its candelabra still lighted under the
arch formed by the stone stairway.—*UKKO *places two glasses and
a jug upon a credenza placed near the fireplace mantel; then,
aided by* HARTWIG, UKKO *brings the two chairs up to the fire.*]

[*The room is now a vast free space where* AXEL *and the* COMMANDER
pace back and forth talking.]

[UKKO *and the three retainers leave by the back of the room.*]

SCENE 9

[COMMANDER, AXEL *alone.*]

COMMANDER [*to himself, watching* AXEL] No, this child does not
even give the least thought either to the royal secret or to its
ultimate mystery on which he could shed some light.—How
can I pluck from him some hint, more important than he
realizes!—Surely, he must know something, without knowing
it! I must . . . gain his confidence entirely before any decision.

AXEL Commander, you have my undivided attention.

COMMANDER [*still to himself*] Let us then be paternal, protective,
the good counsellor! Nothing can ever take the place of old
accepted maxims of wisdom and morality when one wants to
dazzle the inexperienced and facilitate a fatal ascendancy over
them.—The rest, as far as this night itself is concerned, is
decided.

AXEL [*smiling*] Well?

COMMANDER [*aloud*] Ah now!—Now I am speaking quite
seriously,—what in the devil are you doing here, Count, in this
ancient pile, in this forgotten fortress, secluded in the interior
of paradoxical forests, when at the court of any of our kings
a magnificent future awaits you?—You have background, bold-
ness, intelligence; it is criminal for you to fold your arms
among these four walls tumbling into ruin. Move forward! I
summon you to make your way. You are an Auersperg; the
time has come for you to remember it.

81

AXEL [*carelessly*] Let's talk about something else.

COMMANDER Axel, I was very fond of your father ; I must speak on the strength of our old name.—What is the meaning of this blind friendship for your invisible companion, this self-styled " Master Janus "?—Your preceptor, so be it!—He is not a companion to compensate—and he must be gay on winter evenings, if I can give credence to his reputation!—Does one have the right to sacrifice thus the brilliance of an entire line to some vague kind of studies . . .

AXEL [*gravely and simply*] I must warn you that I have transferred my filial respect to the man of whom you are speaking. He was my father's comrade in arms and twice saved his life.

COMMANDER Still, if he were a man really capable . . .

AXEL [*naively*] Capable of what?

COMMANDER In short, you,* a young mind, are wasting your brightest years in these empty investigations of the pseudo-science of Hermeticism!—I have browsed through the titles of the unhealthy volumes of your library. Are you intoxicating yourself with this humid dust? You are letting yourself be indoctrinated by a hallucinated creature who lives in your home. Do you suppose there are still " occult sciences "?—Why it's a candour so very extreme that it verges on the ridiculous, my poor cousin!—If you want to play at medievalism,—go ahead! If so, do it deliberately ; in this way the game is innocent and not even without its grandeur. But to carry the travesty to the point of renewing the breath of the Magnum Opus! by dint of retorts and tubulerous matrasses! to dream of the alloy of mercury and sulphur . . . ah! I still cannot believe it.—Do you know what the liquid gold lying on the bottom of the crucible really is? . . . Your youth. Come away! Send to the devil those worn-out monk's cast-aways which, besides, are not very becoming to a gentleman! Imitate me. Seize life, such as it is, without illusions and without weakness. —Make your way! Go over your course!—and leave the fools to their folly.

---

* The Commander resumes " tu ".

82

AXEL   Cousin, I grant all that you say.—A glass of Hungarian wine?

[*He fills the* COMMANDER'S *glass.*]

COMMANDER   Let me come to the conclusion. I call myself *real life*, do you understand? Is it by exciting the imagination (and this in one of these crenellated manors which no longer make good sense and represent from now on only historical curiosities tolerated for the distraction of travellers) that one can reach something tangible and stable? Get out of this superannuated tomb! Your intelligence needs air. Come with me! I shall guide you there at court where intelligence itself is nothing without flair. Leave the chimera here! Walk on solid ground as a man should. Make yourself feared. Become powerful again. Plunder! You have to succeed! And throw to the nettles and mountain streams this baggage of make-believe at which you would laugh to tears within three weeks if you followed me into royal society. One last time, I beseech you : come make your way. Who can retain you here? You have no secrets, I imagine, neither of money nor of passion! Granted all this, why this absurd exile?

AXEL   [*calmly, sitting down near the credenza*]   My dear, cordial cousin, I am touched—to tears really—by this interest your words bespeak. Your advice comes from a most eloquent man, —and there is no doubt that I should benefit from it in the proper time and place.

COMMANDER   [*to himself*]   What the devil,—the child is undecipherable! . . . What am I to think? Has he really forgotten? Is he inclined to keep quiet by instinctive distrust? And the legend itself, does it perhaps have some foundation? What do I risk if I question him categorically right now? Let him be quiet or let him speak, at least I shall be settled . . . Let's see, let me sound him on the very heart of the matter.

[*Aloud.*]

Then will you let all opportunities for reviving the family glory escape,—you of our eldest branch? And this only for the pleasure of burying your mind in nebulous meditations? Your indifference stupefies me. Positively.

[*A pause.*]

I see that my propositions are something like, say .... like those alleged treasures, you know what I mean—those extra-ordinary riches that my old friend the Count of Auersperg, your father, had the mission to safeguard after our reverses at the time of the French invasion. You know, treasures in hard cash, duly packed in strongboxes, from more than three States of the Confederation!—In short, if I am not duped on this subject by a legend that is an old wives' tale, deliberately embroidered, like so many others, upon a confused but incontestable historical fact, it would appear,—eh? . . . that all that . . . is perhaps not absolutely lost? that the eighty muni-tions wagons of the National Bank of Frankfort were empty when two or three enemy brigades seized them in the heat of that deadly skirmish where your father left his life?—In short, that the four hundred casks of coin and gold bars, not to mention the caissons of precious stones, would not be very far from here? in the environs of this domain,—or something like that? Come now, Auersperg, it seems to me that even a half-certainty of this type merits at least being looked into. Well, what have you tried, attempted, sought, schemed? Nothing, it appears! . . . However, I confess that as far as dreams are concerned, this one was not unworthy of a little attention, because the historical fact, I say, constituted a basis in reality; and, on that basis rested an affair which, *even uncertain but well handled*, could—and can still—become more than advan-tageous for us. Listen! I am your kinsman, your elder, your friend ; our cause is the same ; can't you be open with me? I learned this story, my word, by accident just today. For God's sake, assemble your memories before I leave!—What is there that is strictly true in all that?

[*During this discourse,* AXEL *has watched the* COMMANDER *very intently. He rises and goes to the door at the back of the room.*]

AXEL [*calmly*]   One moment, Commander, I beg of you.

[*Calling.*]

—Herr Zacharias!

[*The* COMMANDER *returns to the fireplace where the high blaze*

84

empurples him in its glare and pours himself a drink.]
[HERR ZACHARIAS *appears at the back of the room.* UKKO *follows him.*]

SCENE 10

[*The same,* HERR ZACHARIAS *and* UKKO.]

UKKO [*aside, smiling, after a glance at* AXEL] Say, lightning is
   going to strike here.
HERR ZACHARIAS My lord called?
AXEL [*in a low voice*] Come here!
[HERR ZACHARIAS *comes to him;* AXEL *looks at him in silence;—
then in a low voice.*]
   You told!
HERR ZACHARIAS [*after a moment*] In the name of your line
   which I have served for eighty years, my lord, I ventured to
   try to salvage the enormous treasure from oblivion before
   dying!
AXEL [*with a frightening expression, leadenly*] Peace be with you!
   [*To* UKKO, *very low*] Two swords. And in a moment have
   Gotthold, Miklaus, and Hartwig here in their old uniforms with
   torches,—and also their old swords. Silence!
[HERR ZACHARIAS *leaves, tottering, by the back of the room.* UKKO
disappears at right after a sign of understanding to the COUNT OF
AUERSPERG.]
[*The end of this scene has passed near the threshold out of*
KASPAR OF AUERSPERG'S *hearing.—During the past few minutes
the storm outside, which had been calmer, resumes its intensity.
The rain begins to rattle on the windowpanes, and there is light-
ning.*]

SCENE 11

[AXEL, COMMANDER,—*then* UKKO *and the three retainers.*]

COMMANDER [*seated with his back turned, warming himself*]
   Count, let's be practical, let's be down to earth.—I shall take

85

it upon myself to be useful and call the attention of the sovereigns of Wurtemberg, Bavaria, and Saxony to the eventuality of a recovery of this incredible vanished wealth. And if, as I want to admit, there is something actually serious at the back of this whole implausible story, I feel confident, listen carefully, in being able to get out of it a more than princely fortune for both of us. A windfall twice miraculous, moreover, because I am ruined, my dear fellow, and the few thousand florins that you agree not to dispute me in the legacy of our late cousin Wilferl of Auersperg, represent for me what a few drops of this golden wine would produce on this red-hot scoop. Come now! Don't you remember some bit of information in talks with your foresters which makes sense now? For example, information regarding some possible means of entry to the ancient subterranean caverns in the mountainous section of the Black Forest? What! this detachment of around two hundred men, circulating in the woods, has not left in the old memories of the countryside any trace of any kind of halt whatsoever, despite such precautions as they may have taken? Have you never heard anything, even something vague, on this subject? never noticed anything in your father's papers . . . in the secret deeds of the house? In the final analysis, it's unheard of! Imagine, being given: (1) the certainty of the preservation of these fabulous securities, and (2) one or two landmarks established by particular or local traditions, there is no doubt that by supporting them with certain calculations familiar to all military engineers, we could obtain credit for five or six million thalers in a few days. And I say that before two months—at the most, three, four even, if you wish,—of constructions and serious excavations in the environs of the fortress, by employing, day and night, if necessary, a thousand of our miners . . . Think of the glorious and lucrative result of that exceptional adventure! There would be a cry throughout Germany! Speak.

[*He turns around and sees the* COUNT OF AUERSPERG *standing, sombre, his arms folded,—at the back of the hall.*]

Well, what is it? What is wrong?

86

[UKKO *re-enters. The young page silently shows his master the two duelling swords which he holds beneath the pommels.* GOTTHOLD *and* MIKLAUS *in their old white cuirassier uniforms, each raising a torch in his left hand and holding a naked sword in his right hand, appear at the back of the hall.* HARTWIG *holds a sword in his only hand. The yellowed horsetail plumes of their casques blend with their white moustaches.*]

[*Silently they station themselves in front of each of the three doors and remain immobile. The* COMMANDER, *a little taken back, looks at them.*]

Now this, why—would it be some fanciful ceremony? . . . Is your "Master Janus" by chance going to have us see some beautiful display of sorcery? It would be a charming gesture. [*He rises.*]

SCENE 12

[AXEL, COMMANDER, GOTTHOLD, HARTWIG, MIKLAUS, UKKO, *then* MASTER JANUS *at the end.*]

AXEL [*coming over to the* COMMANDER *and bowing*] Cousin, a little while ago, you made some remarks which offended me. You are going to give me satisfaction immediately. You cease to be my guest. As a duelling ground, this room is excellent, especially in bad weather.

COMMANDER [*after a pause*] You harebrained . . . , you must be feverish!

AXEL [*continuing*] You have acquired, sir, a reputation as a magistral swordsman in Germany; therefore, the sword will be our weapon.—We shall fight without mercy or truce . . .

COMMANDER [*interrupting*] What! You think that I would give in to the sudden access of dementia which has just stricken the Count of Auersperg?

AXEL [*peacefully finishing his sentence*] To the end: to death.

COMMANDER [*curt and haughty*] On what grounds?

AXEL Oh! very often in the course of travel, one finds himself obliged to take his sword in hand, either at the turning of a main road, or at the end of a small street in a chance town . . . on the grounds of a quarrel without any precise cause,—on the grounds of a simple aggression. I do not have to motivate unduly the abruptness of my provocation, especially in offering you a perfectly regular duel besides.

COMMANDER Bah!

AXEL Judge for yourself. As long as I am standing, you will not leave this room; but since only my presence makes you a prisoner, it will be enough if you hit me grievously for passage to be given you without any other obstacle.—The advantage staying with you, let us suppose, but having cost you some injury, under my roof the same cares would be tendered you as to me.—As soon as recovered, you would be accompanied to the boundaries of this territory without my people showing any sign of resentment.—You cannot take exception to the seconds here present: they are Knights of the Iron Cross;—nor to my page: I vouch for his coming from stock as loyal as it is valorous. These witnesses, then, will keep on their honour and faith, without evasion or subterfuge, the word I pledge you . . . which is that of their lord and friend.

[*He turns around.*]

Take the oath.

[*The lights of the blades and torches which tremble in the veterans' hands make the steel on their cuirasses sparkle. At length all three extend their swords silently.* UKKO, *after an imperious glance from* AXEL, *raises his right hand after an expression of ferocious hesitation.*]

It is sworn.

UKKO [*simply but seriously*] Against my heart.

COMMANDER Am I adequately surrounded?—Ah well! but . . . is your keep a cutthroats' den, cousin?* Let there at least be a sign put up to warn travellers, what the devil! . . . To be sure, I am never known to decline an encounter,—even under conditions like these.—However, how can I take seriously

---

* The Commander uses " vous ".

this tragic actors' show of the most shocking old-fashioned kind? Really, this aims at a certain terrorizing effect which will scarcely faze swordsmen. For my part, I cannot keep from smiling a little.—Believe me, stop this parade as quickly as possible. It would already have become disastrous . . . if I were a child-killer.

AXEL [*impassively*] In the event I should have the unhappy hand, you would take your place below in the family vault. —At the same time I must warn you that on the document notifying the king of your unforeseen decease you would be presumed lost in some mountain stream of these extensive forests.

[*He points to pen, ink, and parchment on one of the crowded black shelves to the right of the fireplace.*]

If therefore you have some dispositions to make, please write them quickly.

[*The* COMMANDER *shrugs his shoulders, folds his arms, and stares at him.*]

No?—That's best.

[*He walks over to* UKKO *who hands him the two swords.—Returning to the* COMMANDER, *he presents the swords by the hilts.*]

Choose.

COMMANDER [*with irritated and arrogant impatience*] Make way for me!

AXEL [*coldly*] Make way for yourself.

COMMANDER [*having seized one of the swords at random,— sullenly*] Prends garde.

AXEL [*calmly*] En garde.

COMMANDER One last time, by the name we both bear I summon you to state precisely your grievances against me.

AXEL [*in a low voice*] Keep the torches high!

COMMANDER You remain silent?

AXEL [*who with sword in hand has moved back to give himself room, answers only with a slight nod.*] Coward!

[*In the lofty hall lightning from the windows blends with the lights of torches and swords.—Distant rolls of thunder.—*AXEL *shudders, then comes over to the* COMMANDER.]

AXEL [*calmly and fiercely*] Look into my eyes carefully.* What sincere contact was ever possible between us but that of swords? Did you think you were touching me when you shook my hand? seeing my real face when I smiled at you? Your improper, destitute speech, I had to tolerate it from a guest seated by my fireside . . . but within myself I was listening to other voices.

However, I heard you as one hears vague animal cries in the distant woods.

—Oh! don't shudder; don't clutch that sword; these are useless affectations in front of us.

COMMANDER [*making the long blade whistle*] Madman! I . . .

AXEL [*impassively*] In a moment. Three times you have challenged me to answer. Don't listen if you don't want to; is it for you alone that I speak? . . . Why should I bother about your inattention—especially when you could not understand me! . . . But consider yourself warned. Your thoughtless boasting has just lost you the right to interrupt me, and if you usurp it from now on, it could be only one more proof of the rash disposition which could, as a consequence, eventually weary my generosity. Therefore, less noise:—let us explain briefly who we are since you have asked.

[*A silence which only the noise of the downpour and thunder disturbs. The* COMMANDER *folds his arms, masking his curiosity by impassiveness.*]

AXEL You who so willingly pronounce another "demented", what proofs of good sense you have given us!—You exhorted me to "look for a fortune" offering yourself as an *example to follow*. Then, a moment later you confessed that you were ruined! . . . Before being so presumptuous, why don't you begin by ridding your own mind of an assumed wisdom which has been able to lead you only to such results?

—On the contrary; you consider yours a mind steeped in "experience", clear-sighted and strong, don't you? And you think that you are always able to dispose of sarcastically the opposing strength of concepts which are inaccessible to you,

---

* Axel now uses "tu".

90

disciplines which are closed to you, discussions of a serene and severe beauty which remain forever boring to you, that is to say, forbidden, since they can seem only futile to you.

However, by what so advantageous subjects of idle conversation do you so often replace the interest which these other subjects, perhaps, encompass? By a grave examination of the spices of a sauce or by canticles on the flavour of a pâté!—Really, however insignificant the object of my favourite studies might be in your judgment, one can hardly see in what respect I have gained in exchange this evening by listening to you.

Let's go on.—Leering at some phantoms through the table glass, you railed at the healthy illusion of my faith in a sole conjugal love,—yes, the only one which merits the name of love.

However, what were you exalting then to the contempt of this pure, youthful, justifiable dream which surely demands first, if not your " respect ",—(which you hardly seem capable of experiencing before anything whatsoever)—at least of your silence?

—Ah! sickening joys: those of vile adultery. So that under the sacred roof of my mother, you made me blush, and so that at the moment I felt almost ashamed before these chaste flowers from the hideous way you smelled them.

For example, you made ring in a high-handed manner, the title of gentleman; you pronounced this word on almost every occasion like a bourgeois.—However, by what proof of generous origin or inner lordliness do you presently justify this idle self-delusion here? . . . You were surprised to see me anxious about a good servant, grown old in my house, and who still walks at this hour lost beneath the storm in the midst of nocturnal dangers to serve me.

Finally, in this dwelling where you deign only to joke about mourning, age, and glory,—when you are indebted solely to the heroism of the ancestors, whose presence has blessed it, for what few good qualities you possess—you proposed to me, if I remember correctly, to follow your lead and subjugate

the integrity of my intelligence and my days to the emptiness
of a thousand laughable intrigues, to go yawn at your side in
a variety of princely antechambers, and you called that
"making one's way". For you it is possible. You are following
the tastes of your nature. It's not the same as mine, that's all.
Let's go on!—My way? It has been laid out for centuries. How
do you presume to make me deviate from it by *your* advice?
Even if my way were among those you dream about, according
to your very confession, zero must be approximately the round
sum and "practical result" where your sagacious and cynical
maxims—empty as nutshells thrown away by monkeys—have
led you as far as position in the State, influence, real considera-
tion, illustrious reknown, and fortune are concerned.—Be less
arrogant and don't call anyone here a madman except yourself.—If you have not been equal to . . . even your mean
ambitions, do not blame fate: it is innocent of your conceited
incapacity . . . unless you wish to make your existence its
crime.

[*The* COMMANDER OF AUERSPERG *gives him a smile of disdainful
indifference. In the midst of incessant flickers of the fireplace,
torches, and flashes of lighting both appear gleaming as if in the
centre of a forge.*]

All right, I know that in the eyes of the majority of human
beings nothing would seem to justify the sudden and shattering
harshness of my words.

[*With a strange smile.*]

Because, in the end, isn't it true? to take pleasure in a welcoming banquet and to say so with verve to one's host while
raising a joyful glass,—to speak fondly of lovely ladies far
away,—to intoxicate oneself delightedly in these aromatic
forest flowers,—to let, once or twice, vibrate in the flight of a
friendly phrase, one's pride in his noble blood,—to confess,
—even without modesty!—that one is little concerned by
ardent concepts and vast thoughts—to recall with a calculated
kindness that sympathy always inspires, the destinies which
seem to be forgotten by one whose youth is already exiled . . .
are these crimes against hospitality? Why have these subjects of

idle talk, so amiable and attractive in themselves, become suddenly between us something so ... sombre?

You assured me of " family friendship ", " sincere understanding ", " tried devotion ", " heartfelt aid ", " experience with royal milieux at my disposal ",* what else? gaiety, brilliant love affairs, and bright lights!—and laughing women at banquets! ... All these words are so captivating because of the intrinsic images which they are supposed to contain and magnetically impart.—Yes, it is true! you uttered them!— even enveloping them with the borrowed elegance of your manner acquired in being around courtiers.

[*Here* COUNT AXEL *is obliged to raise his voice in order to dominate the frightful, increasing fracas of the tempest.*]

But beneath the veil of his subject no one ever translates, evokes, or expresses anything but himself.

Now, conceived by you, imbued with your essence, penetrated by your voice, reflected by your mind, the substances behind these words, because taking root in your nature and being expressed by you, reach me incarnated by your innermost being. They are only so many effigies of you—plucked in the neutral sounds with a vibration always foreign to their meaning and giving lie to it.

For these substances are only supposedly enclosed by words which by themselves can never be more than virtual.—As you conceived them, they no longer seemed to me to have more than a *presumed* identity with those,—of the same name,—of which a living verbal illusion would perhaps have charmed me. Really, how could I *recognize* them? Dry, repulsive, exasperating, fixed,—hostile, from that point on, to the very names which they seemed to usurp on your tongue in order to disillusion me.—When you uttered them, I experienced them stripped of their *real* images, emitting only the odour of a dried heart, only an impression of a cadaverous, immodest soul, only the dull warning of a constantly perfidious ulterior motive. And this threefold element constituted in my eyes the internal

---

* The Commander did not use these precise expressions.

air which you breathe exclusively, hybrid, ambiguous, extinct and tortuous entity that you are; your words reverberated only . . . like confused vocables, translating only the atrophy, innately yours, of the same substances which they presumed to make me desire. So that beneath the heady veils of your talk thus embroidered with these beautiful spectre-words, you should know that you alone,—dismal, florid guest!—appeared to me.

[KASPAR OF AUERSPERG, *his eyebrows scarcely knit but his face very wan, continues to watch* AXEL *silently without unfolding his arms.*]

However, what difference did that make to me! Was *I* your judge! Was it my place to condemn you? to absolve you?— Besides, the hour was already striking for the chamberlain to take up his chain again, to return to his . . . pleasures, to remove from my solitude, in a word, his insignificant shadow. My duty, inherited from my family, became therefore only to conceal completely the deep relief his farewell would bring me. That is why I was going to lead you to my threshold with benevolence and good wishes for your trip. You were to me only a passer-by like the others, having right to deference because of your human form.—Because one pays his respects to the dead!

Suddenly, I perceived that you have made use of your leisure here!—and that you have come upon one of the most important secrets of my house.

[*At these words the* COMMANDER *has started, then regarded the* COUNT OF AUERSPERG *with stupefaction. He looks almost stunned, his mouth half-open.*]

COMMANDER [*shuddering, to himself*] Ah! it's because of that!
. . . Well,—so it's true!

AXEL [*in a rough leaden voice, hoarse at times like a lion roaring*] Really, there you have stirred live ashes. You should have neither inquired nor listened! It's your misfortune to have given way to these temptations. You have lingered like a spy in this lodging.—Since I am the dragon who guards this weighty secret, I shall oppose your noising it about.—Besides, I read in your eyes the intention to assassinate me this very night,—in order to be able to prostitute more effectively this whole great concept of mine in some dubious enterprise.—I was laughing, sure to catch you, at your " departure ". Yes, twice at the table I discerned this fine project in your brilliant transgressor's voice—and beneath my mask of distraction I was spying your low thoughts.

COMMANDER [*tightening his grasp of his sword pommel and speaking almost inaudibly*] What! this braggart plans to arrogate the whole of this overwhelming mountain of gold to himself! . . . Let me first make these soldiers fearful.

[*Composing himself,—then without transition in a flat, clipped voice.*]

Such bombastic insults could awaken only my indifference. I hold a sword—and, in a little while . . . At the same time I must raise objections, of a little less elevated nature, if you don't mind,—since I realize from your remarks that you are outside the law. By inheritance you conceal here a deposit of important national assets. Already criminal from the State's point of view for having kept them out of circulation for so long, you can be summoned by the first German on the scene to restore this treasure to your country, Count of Auersperg! Withholding in this case is stealing.

AXEL [*after a slight start*] Eh . . . Whence comes the austere judge?—At table he vaunted to us with verve those legendary lordly highwaymen whom he proudly called " ancestors " and whose brigandry he extolled.—Now here he is holding a discourse as a man of law and squandering lessons of probity on us. What is the significance of this noble change of front?

COMMANDER [*smiling coldly*] My words were a test—well-founded, it seems. Thus you propose the theft of this deposit entrusted to your filial honour?

AXEL And a little while ago this upright counsellor accused me of never having attempted anything to accomplish the theft. But that was a test, too, I suppose.

COMMANDER Then, dare prove I slander you by restoring to Germany, I say . . .

[*He stops.*]

AXEL [*smiling*]   I dare you to go on!

COMMANDER [*biting his lips a moment*]   Oh! you are required only to reveal officially . . .

AXEL [*after shrugging his shoulders*]   A moment ago it was my duty to restore not only what I do not possess, but what is unlikely even to exist! Now,—simply that I *reveal*—and I am absolved.

[*The* COUNT OF AUERSPERG *before forcing by direct violence the immediate engagement of swords has turned toward the three veterans probably to give some definitive order.*]

[*Suddenly, having looked at them, he starts . . .*]

[*To be sure, the sound of their young lord's indicting outburst has agitated these faithful servants, and in the confusion of sounds they have sometimes even mistaken the cannonade of his words with the bursts of thunderbolts.—The fearful adversary with cold eyes and a hired assassin's voice, how they hate him! Ah! no matter how desperate the combat may be in a little while, they have blind faith in a sure victorious outcome! . . . —However, at the* COMMANDER'S *last words a shadow has fallen over their loyal faces; an anxiety which they have not dared confess among themselves for years, has just entered anew their upright, simple consciences.*]

[*In short, what has just been said, being more within the scope of their humble, rude judgment, appears to them to enclose all the same a grave truth. Out of respect for the infallible and inviolable honour of their young master, they have always refrained from thinking about it. They exchange glances; they would give their life if he would only deign to reply.*]

[*That is why the* COUNT OF AUERSPERG, *who intercepted their glances, has just understood the hidden intention of his adversary at whom he now glares.*]

[*And during the long pause, since the tornado has moved off into the distance, only the sound of rain, torrential and continual, beating against the windowpanes in squalls, can be heard.*]

[*After a violent inner struggle.*]

AXEL   So be it!

[Pointing to the old soldiers with his sword.]

It is because of them, because of them,—alone! do you hear!* that I condescend to answer you on this respectable " legal terrain " when you address me with a view to terrifying these men with the subtleties of a Lorraine notary.—I myself hardly fear the shadow of these bat-wing flutters.

—Soldiers who are our witnesses, put your torches in the wall sockets—and be the judges.

[He goes directly to one of the chairs, sits down, and rests his right elbow on the table which is still lighted. He holds his naked sword full-length between his crossed ankles with his left hand resting on the pommel.]

*[*GOTTHOLD, MIKLAUS, *and* HARTWIG *obey.—Now they are immobile, their right hand resting on their long swords.]*

*[*UKKO *comes to rest his elbows on the back of* AXEL'S *chair.]*

—I affirm that I have the RIGHT to use the treasure as I please in this case with respect to the facts that have just been reproached in my conduct—and I accept the interrogation, since it seems fitting.

COMMANDER *[who has remained standing with sword in hand at the back of the room, impassively]* I was saying, sir, that notifying the State of the treasure is your most elementary duty—at this very instant and before any accidental discovery. For the State grants you your hereditary rights and by protecting them permits you in this case to speak as the master of the treasure. You are a State subject and as such you are bound to notify either its high treasurers, its princes, or, finally, those of its representatives, which by sanctioning in its name the Common Probity, give it form and are its proxies.

AXEL *[cutting off his words very coldly]* Oh! if their counterparts had refrained earlier from having my father massacred in order to regain possession of the Treasury, which they officially entrusted to his sword, for collateral and their entirely personal profit,—and whose treachery nevertheless put his military record at their mercy,—the notorious assets you talk about,

---

* Axel begins using " vous " again.

would have been in legal hands a long time ago. You forget that in this regard I alone have the right to accuse!—Now the State—if those personages were its proxies—is jointly and separately liable for this action. As a result, its Probity which they represent lies dead, perjured, and vain! annulled, if you please! at my threshold . . . It is therefore legitimate enough that the liens of my duty toward this figment of reason,— limited to this calumnious homicide for which they could not indemnify me,—be somewhat relaxed.—This in my opinion is why the gratitude which the spawn of the murderers would presume to inspire in me or impose on me hardly constrains my conscience to authorize . . . were it only one moment of leisure . . . the drawing up of a " memorandum " of a nature to redress for the consorts' joy the awkwardness of a crime.

COMMANDER [*tranquilly*] What! on the contrary, wouldn't this be a signal opportunity for you to bring suit against the State itself in making clear the extremely specious eventuality which is presented? For what motive do you let this opportunity get away?

AXEL [*still curtly and coldly*] The State—which has given me in this case some disconcerting examples,—has permitted itself, still to my detriment, to close this affair definitively by an arbitrary decree which abrogates without appeal even my rights as plaintiff.—From whence in any case I would no longer have to inform it of more or less chimerical hypotheses . . . that it is no longer entitled to hear, that it has forbidden itself to listen to.

COMMANDER You inherit an unfulfilled duty to everyone!

AXEL Come now! Integrity leads you astray! From a soldier who died at his post—no State—and mine in this case less than any other, it seems to me, has anything more to claim! Fulfilled or not, the task is terminated: the child of such a soldier did not inherit the defunct's duties of military service.

COMMANDER [*between deafening claps of thunder*] There are exceptional, unforeseen cases where any gentleman is bound by his nobility alone to defer to the king whose judgment alone is without appeal.

AXEL [*slowly, gravely, bitterly*] You forget what he has pronounced. Who am I in the very words of the king? " The scion of him whose *equivocal and dubious incompetence* lost without hope of recovery the richest royal German treasury ". Verdict rendered on appearances and without inquiry—(with good cause, as we know!)—opposite a name which crowns seven centuries of lofty deeds.—Now even if the king's blotting the escutcheon of this name with such a label did not release me from all deference due the temerarious majesty of him who did not hesitate to offend me with it, I still allege that self-respect no longer permits me send him . . . what could never be a mere unofficial, secret *confidence*. For today the latter would take on implicitly the character of a formal denial of the judgment with which he dared sully heedlessly my father's august memory. Now *upon what* would this denial be founded? Upon *suppositions* of so contestable an authority as my old steward Herr Zacharias? Ah! I maintain that the most ultra-sensitive loyalty in no way obliges me to risk covering myself with such futile ridicule. I have other ways to spend my time.

COMMANDER [*slowly*] So I make a deposition of it, being able with a calculated and serious explanation to enlighten the king—who perhaps would clear the shadow presently cast over your father's name in history,—do you not consent to this?

AXEL A strange pretence of reasoning which has its emptiness exposed by a reflection of the most justifiable prudence! . . . Here in effect, not in dreams, but in fact, is the alternative as far as my filial duty is concerned.

Supposing that after investigation—attempted at great expense on the strength of some dubious legend,—these problematical treasures still cannot be found, there would consequently redound upon the family name only exasperated sarcasm, slurs of disappointed cupidity, ulterior motives increasingly calumnious in my father's regard, especially when we consider the new publicity given his death.—The universal error could only be deepened.

Supposing that the treasure was suddenly recovered. Inasmuch as its discovery would entail inevitable disgrace—and the most " inopportune " scandal—that is the affair would surely harm the public security, confidence, and honour in their most " official " representatives, here is approximately the tenor of what—on the testimony of the Past in its entirety— the Rule of State, which overrules all equity in causes of that order and which you refrain from mentioning, would automatically dictate to History. Here is what posterity would learn:

We shall never know to what end the General of Auersperg, a few days before falling into enemy hands, took upon himself— surrounding his moves with confusing and disconcerting precautions—to bury in the most secret part of one of his most remote domains, the immense wealth under discussion. History could not begin to establish the motives which led him thus to conceal the liquid assets of Germany.—However, his son, AXEL OF AUERSPERG, *by his noble restitution was able to redeem what paternal inconsistency in this case offers of the irregular and even strange,—and which had once darkened the blazon hitherto unspotted, of that illustrious family.*

Yes: such would be the radiant addition of reknown to result from my refurbishing the memory of my heroic father. Now, my filial piety, more sagacious than your advice, warns me that in such circumstances it would not be EVEN in my family interest to exhume this cause.

COMMANDER And persuading yourself of these paradoxical subtleties you acquiesce by a singular absention to the *fait accompli* of error which dishonours his ashes? when, I repeat, a quite simple communication to the Privy Council could, in spite of your contradictory predictions, render to your name, which is mine also, all its past honour!

AXEL Oh! among *my people,* sir, we have never needed anyone to decree our honour, since the fatherland, founded across the centuries by our acts and those of our peers in the military nobility owes to us the purest part of its own honour ... —No one whatsoever could be entitled to verify the honour of those whose living function is to penetrate in a real sense that of other

100

men. And we are rather unconcerned about the valueless esteem of random passers-by (however numerous we suppose them to be) who presume to dispute it even once. I do not have to take account of your last proposals. I am here in my hereditary home, an exile's hearth in a place of exile, the fatherland being no more than a piece of ground to me. I do not have to worry about what may be interred in the environs of this dwelling since my father did not leave me a memorandum on that subject. Since no law forces me to concern myself with it, no one whatsoever could contest my RIGHT to reject the responsibility for it.

COMMANDER   Your father left to you even less the duty of confiscating in this manner the well-being of several million innocent people. In the name of a grievance you think you have against a certain few, you use the pretext of an omission of the Law in order to make all feel the weight of a resentment as fanatical as unjust.

AXEL [*smiling*]   Really, at this moment the least experienced financier in the tiniest state of the West would simply stare at you in silence: because it is astonishing to hear a courtier demonstrate such deep-seated ignorance. If your notions on the nature of Gold are limited to that of spending it, they spare my having to answer you.

COMMANDER [*impassively, without understanding*]   A gravely uttered evasion hardly affects one who defends the common interest.

AXEL   The common interest! By the consensus of centuries that generous motto has been used by princely plunderers to justify the exactions of their good pleasure; it still permits extorting the plebeians' benediction while coldly despoiling them in the very name of their interest.—No, in this case, I do not have to invite the common champions of " common interest " to pillage.

COMMANDER [*coldly*]   Well, if because of these specious motives, it does not please you to notify the States concerned on your own initiative, let others assume the care and responsibility of it, and we shall come soon to free you from this gold—which you do not value and which it not yours anyway.

101

AXEL [*calmly and haughtily*] Being able to oppose it, why should I permit one or two thousand brutes in your pay to appear here suddenly, to profane over a long period of time by show of force, by the gross mockery of their presence, the only place of exile where I may enshroud the dignity of my life? I know that it can seem quite simple to men of law, that in the name of that "common interest" that wretched lie which has just come into the discussion,—under the pretext, in short, of reconquering the gold which is perhaps imaginary,—it may be lawful for columns of excavators to come deface this land, prize of the glorious blood of the whole race vested at last in me,—and to plunder this soil which my family trampled as dutiful sons for centuries. What right would my sentimental attachments have! Could I be indemnified for these thousands of old trees, old friends of mine, once they were felled and uprooted?—No. The silence of the great forest—the march of which I am the margrave—is not for sale. It is a sacred trust which I do not mean to have expropriated and which could not be indemnified by the gold of your banks. And even if the alleged improvement of the "well-being" of a million unimportant people were to follow, I say that on the same scales such pebbles would vainly try to outweigh a precious stone,—and that this well-being would not equalize in real EQUITY the defraudation inflicted upon me.

COMMANDER Whom will you convince that such a treasure is not worth the seeking, even if it were at the price of total silence?

AXEL [*disdainfully*] Myself alone; that should be enough. I think that I have proved for some time that this task would not have been difficult.—For example, it is quite likely that *you* would prefer Gold (even if it were only fictitious) to total silence,—since Silence means only yawning to you. Indeed, this word, empty when you usurp the right to pronounce it, has not (even with the same syllables) a trace of a relationship with the word as I have uttered it just now. It is futile for you to try to confuse them in the same valuation . . .

[*Smiling.*]

102

Like a forger or a parrot.

COMMANDER [*impassively*] In short, if, thanks to some paternal clue unexpectedly brought to light, you should happen to discover these enormous deposits, what *then* would be your duty in your eyes?

AXEL [*tranquilly*] To bury them still further underground, if I could, out of respect for the Poor.

COMMANDER [*after a pause*] Flippancy of brief duration once your age of discretion is tolled.

AXEL [*gravely*] I doubt whether that age is ever to be tolled for you.

COMMANDER All right. You consider yourself free, apparently, to annul knowingly the act of a man who deposited these national fiscal resources in his grounds to assure better their temporary security—so as to be able in the end to return them in their entirety to the etablished powers of Germany when the moment arrived!

AXEL And it was his fatal moment that the established powers of Germany made arrive. Therefore, wherever the treasure may be, here or elsewhere, does not concern me! Let it sleep! Surely I at least share with everyone else the right to ignore it. Thanks to the deadly duplicity of your representatives, no one knows what has become of your Gold. Germany has prescribed my legitimate rights of inquiry into the event which would explain and expose the disappearance. Time has expatiated upon the story, already ancient . . .—So be it.

COMMANDER [*impassively*] In conclusion, you are aware of the origin of the wealth buried—to my satisfaction at any rate— beneath your land! Annulling them in this way is still disposing of them; *now,* what right can you invoke for this decision?

AXEL That of safeguarding their oblivion.

COMMANDER Under what title?

AXEL [*rising, calmly and sombrely*] Under the title signed in blood which covers them—and paid for them.

[*After a brief pause.*]

I shall add, however, one thing you have not questioned me about. In Germany there are so many miserable people,

whose distressing hunger—that's your people's work!—makes
me nauseated to look at you.—It would be somewhat base
to forego completely the right of helping them,—in the event
where, for example, the Gold we're discussing would offer
itself ABSOLUTELY as a godsend.

In short, struck from memoranda, prescribed by official decrees,
renounced by its indemnified claimants, a hundred years
really could have passed over it without franchising it more
completely. What is left? a legend.—If the treasure still
exists, imagination makes it into a blazoned mine—lying, no
one knows where, beneath the Forest. This unclaimed wonder
is thus at the mercy of whoever is predestined for it, if he is
led to it by a decree of that Necessity who watches over
man's fate. Yes, its *legal* heir will be the first traveller who—
when the earth gives way beneath his steps—will make his way,
staggering and blind, into the passages where these dormant
riches glow. Why? Because he will receive his investiture only
from Fate, their unique *proprietor* today.

Well! no written communication will deliver to me the secret
of the cavernous spot, vaulted with soil and shadow, where
sleeps the imperial German treasure. My father has not
appeared to reveal it to me. If, therefore, it offered itself to
me without warning, without my having been guilty of a single
effort of search,—that is, having achieved for myself also the
status of a mere passer-by,—what pretence of bitter remorse
or what false scruples would justify my not heeding my royal
duty to defend its value from the low use by which so many
living men would not fail to profane it foolishly? Why should
I refuse from Destiny—from whom I certainly accepted life!
the burdensome new gift it would seem to put in my
charge? Let me repeat, since I have not made any attempt
to conquer this heritage although I know it to be here, I
should feel divinely marked to seize it if it came to me from
the depths of the Unknown. Immense as it might possibly
appear to me then, in all its shining horror, I maintain that
for me it would be . . . like a lost purse that a pilgrim
stumbles over in the road in the evening,—at a time, however,

when his eyes were intent upon the stars alone!

COMMANDER I think simply this, myself,—that the underground belongs to the State:—so, if, having wind of this grave secret, they sent here a few companies of the army engineering corps, you would be obliged indeed to let the State retake its wealth because its squads would hardly be receptive to the sublimity of your concepts.

MIKLAUS, HARTWIG, *and* GOTTHOLD [*with short, sonorous, brief laughs*] Oh, ho!

UKKO [*with a slight shrug of his shoulders*] Too bad I don't feel like laughing.

AXEL [*to the* COMMANDER] A delusion!—Not a pick would strike here, not one of those wretches would leave the neighbourhood alive. And . . . it is solely to avoid the pestiferous emanations which their useless slaughter could emit that I prefer precisely to kill you alone.

COMMANDER Oh, come now, I must be dreaming! You would attempt a rebellion against the Law? against the State? against the king?

AXEL [*gravely disdainful*] From a military point of view I alone know what extensive danger, what deadly ambush this Forest hides and can suddenly present, for we have commanded here for three centuries! Four or five hundred soldiers, dispatched upon this terrain would not make twenty leagues through the woods toward this keep before a simple accidental catastrophe would make the ground they covered give way beneath them, entombing them—making them like the Gold they had come seeking.—Result: when such incidents would thwart the initial stages of an enterprise, vague and dubious to begin with, those in command would argue over risking new offensives for such hazardous benefits. Time would pass in indecision, vain investigation, commentary; uneasy forgetfulness would move in . . . —in short the *status quo* would remain by virtue of my hidden will.

COMMANDER Granted that you did not know what several hundred disciplined men, a thousand if need be, wisely led, can do,—would your conscience coldly resolve on this criminal madness?

105

AXEL [*smiling*]   In this case I have no more accounts to render; upon this point I cannot admit a judge. Approval, condemnation, stupefaction would find me equally unmoved.—In my " conscience " I alone am qualified to deliberate. I decide : — and everything is said.

COMMANDER   These shameful convictions are merely inhuman, sir, and this is nothing to be proud of.

AXEL [*rising*]   You are free to attempt—vainly—to believe it. —But since the value of your motives has been reduced to zero, the debate is closed.—And we shall not clutch the iron in our fists for further discussion.

[*Seeing the* COMMANDER OF AUERSPERG *smile at this speech, he continues abruptly—ferocious again.*]

Ah! I see that, protected by our sworn oath, you* trust blindly in your skill with this weapon. My oath ought to prove to you what counter-faith I also must cherish since I want to consecrate by the mysterious blood of law-abiding combat, my rights to silence and oblivion,—especially when it would be so legitimate for me to annul you without risk.—Well, I predict : you will not get away from my sword alive. Why, it will be like duelling thunder. I am going to suppress you without anger, the way I should kick a stone from my path,— without your death interrupting in my mind the course of a single of those thoughts—more lofty than any concerning us now—which are beyond your ken. You are a nullity, and I shall nullify you without fear of a single moment of remorse. I have no grudge against you; I do not see you. As far as I am concerned you are inanimate : you are the eternal moth which by his own impulse has flown hither to destroy himself in the eternal flame—With this, you are herewith warned. I have spoken.

COMMANDER [*to himself*]   Oh! I want to learn something else before killing him!

[*Aloud, coldly.*]

---

* Axel begins to use " tu ".

You have diverted me, you are overtired;* this is the only thing clear in your harangue. Let's put an end to it. You wish to withhold from various German States absolutely untold sums and I am in your way. All right. In this conjuncture, Count . . .

[*He disdainfully drops his sword.*]

I will not fight. I really do not have to do this honour to thieves,—even when they are in my own family.

AXEL [*tranquilly and gravely, in loud voice*] If my too helpful father had not accorded you** once, from weariness, the honour of touching his hand—and recognised your kinship (his absent-minded indulgence has protected you the past two hours),—I should have done justice earlier to this bad faith, effrontery, empty imprudence:—let's end it.

[*Pacific, as if making a quite ordinary announcement.*]

My fortress was the military key of a German march. An imperial rescript vests the suzerain of this place with the rights of martial law even in time of peace.

[*To* UKKO, *pointing to the carabine.*]

Therefore, in the name of that hereditary mandate, take up that gun; aim at that man's heart and—if he does not raise his sword instantly,—fire!

[UKKO *rushes to the wall, seizes the weapon, fingers the lock, and returns to stand three paces from the* COMMANDER. *He quickly rests his cheek and arm in firing position.*]

COMMANDER [*paler, aghast*] Up in Prussia people know that I am here. You*** will have to render account of your acts and your remarks. To justify an assassination you argue from a dead letter, a feudal decree abrogated by disuse. You feign to be unaware of the century we live in.

AXEL [*indifferently*] Oh! have yourself dated tomorrow, if you wish. *I am.*

COMMANDER [*with a tremor of cold fury*] Leave that out! You

---

* The Commander uses " tu ".

** So Axel uses " vous ".

*** The Commander uses " vous ".

are the one who speaks only of *yesterday,* being heedless of *tomorrow.* I, sir, am glad to be a man endowed with some reason, to date only from the century in which I exist,—to be solely a man of *today.*

AXEL   Then, be careful: it is late.

COMMANDER [*still under control, but shuddering, nearly inaudibly*] To see myself obliged to knock this solemn fanatic down to the floor, when by reporting his words to the king, I could get any handful of police guards with a simple writ of extradition to come here at once to this tumble-down hovel and carry him away muzzled to a fortified prison!

UKKO [*in an undertone*]   A signal and I fire, my lord.

COMMANDER [*folding his arms recklessly*] Well, go ahead, murder me!—or by your pledged word, reply clearly to this supreme question: *Where am I and who are you?*—Only this time, be precise, exact, and clear, dear sir. Out in the world we barely esteem phrase-makers.

AXEL [*after a start of impatience*]   Down here we do not prefer small-talkers. Ah! you* dare defy me to fulfill *more* than my promise because of your curiosity.

[*Sombrely.*]

Well,—you will be satisfied.

[*To* UKKO.]

Raise your weapon a moment. Three times this chamberlain has threatened us with his kings, his men of arms, and the like,—it seems that the tail of this peacock folds up to show the keys embroidered on the back of his peaceful uniform. Really, all this, in the end brings on vertigo! Let him learn then *where he is and who I am :*—I swear that he will not have time to forget it.

[*He takes his sword by the hilt, goes up to the* COMMANDER, *who watches him with folded arms—and touches him on the shoulder with the pommel.*]

—You ** are in this unique Forest where nighttime reigns

---

* Axel uses " tu ".

** Now Axel uses " vous ".

for a hundred leagues. It is populated by twenty thousand foresters with dangerous carabines,—veteran soldiers born from stock that has owed me fealty for generations.—From my central location I watch over it from a very old stone pile which already has driven back three sieges.

From the brink of my moat to the furthest outskirts, villages and hamlets are under my command;—scarcely five days would be necessary for all of them, at the same time, to be informed of an order sent out from these walls,—say a memorandum! because if one is loved ever so little, a memorandum succeeds better than an order, and in these woods hearts have become so primitive again that you yourself would not find a traitor. What difference would it make anyway! Any happening *which affects me,* whether by one or many, is soon signalled to me.—Depending upon the size of the adversary, we forearm and stand ready at all approaches. Once into the successive stretches of the Forest, how can you live, orient yourself, shelter yourself from the night, in short, advance without being seen? Without my direct help,—would you have made your way here? No. Indeed, several days before you presented yourself here, I had wind of two horsemen . . .

[*Catching himself and turning his clear gaze upon the* COMMANDER.]
And even a—woman . . .

[*A pause:—then to himself—as if having definitively settled a doubt in view of the* COMMANDER'S *attentive impassiveness.*]
—(They do not know each other.)

[*Resuming coldly the broken sentence.*]
. . . were making their way to my dwelling. They were closely watched and overheard.—So I sent you guides who brought you to my threshold in fewer than six days.—You spoke a moment ago about a "picket of policemen",* dispatched to this keep with a writ of *habeas corpus?* . . . What would be left of them, soon lying beneath the green branches at my good pleasure,—if, on the contrary, I did not have

---

* The Commander has not used this expression.

them guided in their turn as far as my drawbridge—lowered before them in the name of the king?—Well! they would enter,—and with an air of authority most likely!—into the casern court of this castle . . .—Then, without inconveniencing even a single servant . . .

[*He walks to the casement and opens it—and, with a blast of his hunting whistle, pierces the shadows and pounding rain.*]
[*Horrifying barking and a fracas of chains resound; countless repercussions of heavy bodies hurling themselves against a massive door can be distinguished.*]

. . . yes, I have there, your hear? thirty Ulm dogs of the great tawny breed, war dogs. This ferocious pack, obeying me alone, serves me in night hunting; it beats the game thickets around me in the Forest unceasingly. In a few moments it would leave your men mere blood-drenched bones on the grass and paving stones.—To be sure, knowing the rules of the game, I should deplore this episode loudly,—of such unforeseen suddenness . . . that I had no time to avert it,—no time even to learn the *object* of the deputation!—And I should formally scold my dogs in front of all the castle personnel, because I certainly don't want to pass for a rebel! . . . Only, I think that after two or three of these mishaps, they would stop sending me such visitors.—Spare us then these puerile threats which amuse these old soldiers and this youngster.

At the slightest indication, at the merest presentiment of murderers sent against me—and, as I just said, they would undoubtedly perish in some ravine during the first stages,— I would take the offensive, since I should have to consider the princes, acting in this way against me, as simple aggressors in a duel where their chosen weapon was assassination. —No, I should not be one to decline the preferred weapon of such kings. Besides, would not they be sons of those founders of all dynasties who one day in the distant Past revolted against their sovereigns also and supplanted them? —I should endeavour to prove myself a peer of their ancestors (on this point at least) and render myself thus worthy of the *honour* they do me, knowingly or not.

110

Actually I have at my command several sure defence measures. In my control throughout the Forest I have a host of miners with sturdy arms and rough faces, who remember the enforced army conscription of their youth and whose shoulders still bear the furrows of scars not entirely healed by time. No one besides me can realize fully how their old resentment, totally in force, toughens in their veins when they work their way through the depths of the subterranean galleries with their picks clutched in their fists while they brood over your amiable princes.—Being sent as executioners into a particular capital to lie in wait day after day for that moment when a deadly, well-aimed bullet can fell a king would fire them with a drunkenness that is their sole thirst—one they would cheerfully quench at your usual hangman's price. You will surely admit that I have enough gold to defray them in such enterprises—and that I could even conceive the overall plan for a " regicide ", as you say in town, so that their safe return might be more than likely. Therefore, I have every ground for still maintaining that after two or three of these warnings or coincidences the august successors of my crowned antagonists would not disturb my solitude further . . . this all the more because with my pitiless perseverance I should not be the first to weary.

Let us suppose, for example,—(shouldn't we consider every eventuality?)—that at the suggestion of some counsellor like you, some head of state of one of these German " fatherlands ", exasperated finally by several costly and ominous failures,—cannot tolerate the constant humiliation of his formal orders,—and perhaps with some suspicions also about these " revolting " facts begins to distrust more astutely not only me but my silent entourage,—let us suppose, I say— since, after all, we could not possibly imagine how far a prince's " indignation " might lead him!—that this legal king should suddenly dispatch rather heavy forces—eight or ten thousand men, for example—with orders to effect a military occupation of the Black Forest, to raze my walls and to bring

111

me back, dead or alive! This solely so that "Force may reside with the Law".

In the name of human Rights I declare that to make war on a solitary exile guilty merely of legitimate defence, silence, and liberty—firmly decided in any case to safeguard his isolation, even to blow up his bastion rather than surrender,—yes, I maintain that to make war on that man would be an act worthy of the derision of History, the contempt of nations,—and would bring dishonour to the country.

Never mind! . . . Thanks to those ancestors of mine who—through many years of hereditary patience which I am demonstrating right now—have armed my keep, I am ready to defy those bellicose phantasies. Being from a warrior race and knowing the exact amount of terrain a corps of ten thousand men, divided into columns of assault, attack, and support, can occupy *here,* my dispositions have been taken for a long time.

[THE COUNT OF AUERSPERG *resumes his seat and leans near the table lights.—For a few minutes the fracas of the thunder, the swirling gusts of the diluvial storm seem to have closed in as if to grasp the heights of the fortress in one supreme battle.*]

First, you should know that around me the mountainous and wooded terrain would obstruct all military offensives. In short, there are on all sides, at a distance, wide, circular valleys, torrential rivers, countless boulders,—and enormous trees which are pressed so close together that if they were sawed at their base, they would prop one another up without falling ; besides, their fall would block the advance of an army.—To engage cannon in the midst of such countryside with the view of fighting me in the breach would demand really extremely heavy—and actually fruitless—sacrifices of blood, time, and gold . . . even just to be driven back. No cavalry could move in this region,—for the military maps, rectified from time to time according to new practices, are in my hands *alone.* Let me add that because of this knowledge I should not have waited for a surprise eruption of enemy regiments. Other means would be necessary to attack me.—Only extensive foot troops, set loose in the boundless Forest would *seem* to be able to reach the approaches to my trenches out there, although with difficulty and in disorder, under my continual direct fire covering all fortifications.

For the crenellations (which you've overlooked) of this medieval castle were provided in earlier times with forty-eight siege pieces, oh! still in shining order. And, if called for, they would be operated, even if it were tomorrow, by a garrison of rough veterans familiar with them.—From the height which this fortress dominates, their powerful plunging fire covers a zone of more than two leagues, and the support area of this zone is kept constantly in condition to furnish to this side of the trenches entirely adequate supplies of bread, staples, water, even ammunition. As for my casemates, their storerooms stay provisioned for a long resistance as in the past.

That is why no act of authority, revealing my real power, would betray my overt revolt at the beginning of hostilities. —Nothing. The interminable stretches of trees, ruts, precipices, and ditches would keep first their rural aspect, then their wild aspect,—and the first lines of infantry, penetrating the forest, would hear from village to village only the wheel of the ropemakers, the axe of the woodcutters, the peaceful hammer of the shoemakers, the murmurs of streams, the lullabies sung by women at the cradle. Nothing would denote resistance or danger. According to the roads chosen, I should probably not have to take new measures from this manor until a line five or six leagues from my trenches was reached. —In short, why put those people I could call mine into maneouvres before they are of necessity attacked themselves and the Forest becomes a little more sinister? When the first fortified town is molested by arriving troops, all of their own accord would fall back here! For the defence of the Forest we have a formation completely unknown to your soldiers and which would crush them,—annihilate them, even, I am well assured of it!—So that suddenly on some black night during the weary sleep of your thousands of men, here are glades become furnaces, and in the suffocation of the burning woods the mine bursts would intersperse the crackle of thousands of carabines, and dawn would shine on simple, thorough slaughter. In winter this would be more brief and more terrible still because in these terrains, worked since olden times, I maintain means of producing widespread landslides for burying people alive—and being able to use those millions of combatants which do not retreat, I mean the trees, I know how to starve, render piecemeal, in short neutralize forces . . . which, besides, would be far from being, in any respect, equal to those I would command.—By simulating defeat, say, there are two paths which could lead the assault columns up to my green plateaus and moat. From their summit I can not only plummet colossal rounded boulders which would inevitably crush them, but, thanks to old wartime tunnels which go along the summit, I can make a landslide giving these paths such an incline that . . . would render this old keep completely impregnable,—and with simultaneous steady fire which would be the finishing touch. In my opinion it would be chimerical speculation to try to estimate the number of deserters who—without shelter, guides, provisions, lost in the woods,—tracked to death by my people, would try to gain the outskirts to go carry the news of the alarming disaster to their country.—This disaster would soon be followed by a surprise attack on some nearby fortified city, by a call to discontented domains, and, without any doubt, by a civil war in Germany. At the outcome of one or two battles carried out by a plan of hostilities already perfected, I know which criminal prince I would remove.

—MY RIGHTS would remain intact; because . . . was it *I* who made me an outlaw?

This is the very place where you are, Lord Chamberlain. As for *me,* I am quite simply a rather bothersome visionary whom it would perhaps behoove your kings not to challenge. For example,—(to put an end to talk between us now, right?)—you have, I imagine, already heard . . . of a young man of former days, who, from the depths of his castle of Alamont

114

built on that Syrian plateau referred to as the *Roof of the World*, used to force distant kings to pay him tribute.—They called him, I believe, the Old Man of the Mountain?—Well . . .

[*At a signal* GOTTHOLD *and* MIKLAUS *have taken up their torches again;—*AXEL *rises, glowing in the red reflections of the entire hall, looks at his adversary, and says in a tranquil voice.*]

. . . well, *I* am the Old Man of the Forest.

[COMMANDER, *a little haggard, but having become graver, eyes him from head to foot as if to give himself countenance*] Rebel! You dare to take—such rights! . . .

AXEL [*his eyes afire*] No one ever had other rights than those he took and—knew how to keep.—And, you may be sure, I intend to take them all! at the first conspiracy of your masters.

COMMANDER [*watching him, in low voice*] Being able to become king, why not be one?

AXEL [*pointing with his sword to the sword lying on the flagstones*] I have other things to think about.

[*A profound silence.*]

COMMANDER [*with a pale, icy smile, as if resigning himself to the inevitable*] Obviously, you twist my words to suit yourself! Let's get on with it! let's cut each other's throats: so be it.

[*He stoops to pick up his sword, then in a strange voice.*]

It would be more correct to remove our coats, I think.

AXEL [*without even noticing the low, suspicious meaning of these words*] Granted.

[*Sticking their swordpoints in the floor, both hastily disrobe to the waist—throwing their clothing on the two chairs. Their muscular physiques appear: that of the* COUNT OF AUERSPERG, *svelte, athletic, and rippling; that of the* COMMANDER, *robust, agile, resistant. Seizing their weapons again, they back five or six paces away from each other in the centre of the room.*]

COMMANDER [*in a firm, curt voice*] Soldiers of the Iron Cross, I, Hermann Kaspar of Auersperg, baron of his Majesty our King, Commander in the Order of the Red Eagle, I take you as my witness that I have protested against the arbitrary conduct of Count Axel of Auersperg, my cousin, who, exceeding in my

115

regard all bounds of threats, boasts, and outrages, puts me in the urgent and absolute necessity of trying to take his life.

[*With a glance he examines the terrain of the room.*]

AXEL [*in a low voice, smiling*] Lofty words: when the action?

COMMANDER [*sword raised*] This time *I* am waiting for you, sir.

AXEL [*tranquilly, assuming en garde*] Here I am.

[*The two adversaries, coming together rapidly, engage only the forepoints of their blades. The attacks of the* COMMANDER OF AUERSPERG *succeed one another hurriedly with the trigger quickness of superior speed and skill.* AXEL, *reserved, has met him as many times, the irons in shocks hard enough to cause sparks. Several minutes pass thus.*]

[*Now the swords, as if mutually informed and evaluated, no longer meet. Deceiving each other in close feints, they outguess and elude each other. They seem to be two shimmering lights, continually rejoining and mirroring beneath the torchlight, interlacing without contact, almost without noise.—Suddenly, two thrusts, seemingly mortal, but met at their very flash by the young count's thorough guard, come quickly at him. For the past several minutes as the blades are intercrossing,* AXEL *has not extended his arm once.—Outside thunder bursts at every instant.*]

COMMANDER [*to himself, breaking pace, on the brink of a bitter surprise*] Ah! but . . . I feel—that I am losing.

[GOTTHOLD'S *eyes, anxious until now, have followed the duel and translated the retreats of the feints. He lights up seeing the* COUNT OF AUERSPERG *quickly advance one pace at the* COMMANDER'S *break and draw aside in a manner undoubtedly significant to the old soldier.—*UKKO, *arms folded, very pale, looks on near* MIKLAUS, *whose torch trembles; at the back of the hall* HARTWIG, *his hand clutching his sword, has shut his eyes because an anxious tear has just fallen upon his moustache.*]

[*Meanwhile the* COMMANDER *multiplies his dangerous, precise, skillful thrusts at* AXEL, *making with his sword point a minute, scarcely visible pattern.* AXEL *stays like a stone statue in the shelter of his moving wrist, secluding himself in impenetrable swordplay.*]

[*Suddenly, after evading a clash—which a trace of irritated*

116

fatigue has momentarily exaggerated,—AXEL *lunging with the force of a wild beast, unbends with a countering guard position to bring his arm and iron into one straight line : suddenly drops of blood spurt in the air between the two combatants. The* COM- MANDER KASPAR OF AUERSPERG *utters a short, raucous cry which leadenly smothers itself;—he turns on himself, beats the air with his two arms, letting his weapon escape, then staggers. His knees bend; he falls forward on his two outstretched hands.—Soon, face against the flagstones, he writhes, then remains motionless; in three seconds a wide red pool forms and increases at his left side.*]

UKKO [*who rushes up, raises him, turn him over, feels the wound*] The heart is pierced. It is all over.

[*A pause.*]

AXEL [*to himself, thoughtfully, considering his adversary, already inert*] Passer-by, you* have passed away. Here you are sinking down into the Unthinkable. During your days of narrow self-sufficiency you were nothing but a dross of animal instincts refractory to all divine selection! Nothing ever *called* you from the Beyond! And you have fulfilled yourself. You fall to the depths of Death like a stone into a void,— without attraction and without goal. The speed of such a plunge, multiplied by the single ideal weight, at this point is . . . immeasurable . . . so that this stone in reality *is no longer anywhere.*—So disappear! even from between my eyebrows.

[*Aloud, turning toward the three old soldiers.*] Come here.

[GOTTHOLD *and* MIKLAUS *come up.—Bent beneath their torches, they look at the body stretched out on the floor.* UKKO, *his hands bloodied, holds the livid face on his knees.*—HARTWIG *rushes up from the back of the hall to look also.*]

[*Long naked swords gleam around the dead man.*]

—Thank you, my old friends, for the anxiety your tenderness has suffered!—Send someone to reassure Herr Zacharias.

---

* Axel uses " tu " with the corpse.

[*Pointing to the* COMMANDER OF AUERSPERG'S *body.*]

    —To the tomb crypts—this very night!

GOTTHOLD [*in* AXEL'S *ear and protecting his words with his hand because of the deafening roars of thunder which now strike the summit of the keep*]   A grave is ready, my lord. It was yours, —dug once at your express desire . . .

AXEL [*impassively*]   So be it: his ashes for mine.

[*He lets his half-reddened sword fall.*]

[*A moment earlier the arched door at the top of the stone stairway silently opened in advance of an unknown personage.*]

[*The newcomer is of tall stature with admirable proportions. His pure-featured physiognomy does not seem to belong to a man of our times or our lands; it recalls strangely those hieratic or royal likenessess in relief upon very ancient Medean medallions. He appears to be in his fiftieth year, although the radiance of his grave eyes attests some powerful, eternal corporeal youth. The austere beauty of his whole person, the luminous pallor of his face, the magnificent expression of his glance seem as if they must subjugate the memory even of those who look on him only once.*]

[*His wavy brown hair, slightly silvered, only a little longer than is worn in the army, is parted over a mysterious brow whose plenitude imposes peaceful contemplation. His brown beard recalls those of faces found engraved on Nineveh brasses. Flashes of lightning illuminate him.*]

[*His costume, almost a black uniform without a sword, appears at first to be that of Hungarian army doctors; but several details of a completely severe simplicity indicate instead that it is the clothing of a horseman always ready to go on a long journey.— A wide-brimmed hat and cloak complete his costume.*]

[*At the moment he descends into the room,* GOTTHOLD *and* MIKLAUS, *aided by* UKKO, *have raised the* COMMANDER OF AUERSPERG'S *lifeless body, and, preceded by* HARTWIG *whose torch lights their way, they proceed toward the centre door.—*THE COUNT OF AUERSPERG *has just put on his clothes again, and as he finishes belting his burnished leather jerkin, the unknown man, now on the first steps, appears before him.*]

AXEL [*to himself*]   Master Janus.

[*A pause. Then with a deep sigh.*]
   Ah! in the presence of this living being I feel that I have
become a mere man once more.

PART III
THE OCCULT WORLD

Welcome your thoughts like guests
and your desires like children.

Lao-tse.

I

At The Threshold

[*The same room.*]

SCENE 1
[AXEL, MASTER JANUS.]

AXEL [*preoccupied, gloomy*] Master, that was a man I killed.

MASTER JANUS [*lighting one of the ancient clay lamps*] So be it.

AXEL [*in a low voice, almost to himself*] For a secret . . . which
I do not know,—which yesterday I had forgotten,—and which
has obsessed me for an hour.—I thought I was free from the
thralldom of curiosity which subjugates me once again.

[*He opens a folio volume on one of the shelves—he gives up
trying to read.*]

—My soul is so distracted it finds strange even these luminous
words which have dazzled me so many times.—I am undone!
Something has happened which has called me back to earth.
I can feel it: I want to live! . . .

MASTER JANUS [*to himself, as he studies* AXEL *in the lamplight*]
Then you* are ripe for the supreme Test. The vapour of the
blood shed for the Gold has just diminished your essence.
The fatal effluvia envelope you, penetrating your heart—and,
under their pestilential influence, you have become a child
again, stammering mere words. Heir to the instincts of the
man you killed, you live through the old thirsts of voluptuousness, power, and pride, inhaled and reabsorbed into your
organism, lighting up the reddest blood in your veins. O
redescended from the sacred thresholds, the former mortal is
going to come back to life in the disavowing eyes of the
guilty Initiate! The Hour has come—She too is going to come,
she who renounced ideal Divinity for the secret of the Gold,
as you are going to renounce presently your sublime finalities

---

* Master Janus uses " tu '.

for this contemptible secret. Here then face to face the final
duality of the two races 1 chose from the depths of the ages
*that simple and virginal Humanity might conquer the two-fold
illusion of Gold and Love,*—that is, to found in a point of
Becoming the virtue of a new Sign.

AXEL [*to himself, in a low voice*]   It seems to me that I am awaking from a chaste, pale dream, dreamt in diamond-coloured
ethers leaving a memory which is going to fade away. Until now
I had seen only the light of the world of enchantment which
this man unveiled for me; at this moment I see only its darkness. An immense doubt encompasses me . . . Life calls to my
youth, stronger than these concepts which are too pure for
the fiery season ruling me! That dead man ensnared me . . . the
blood perhaps . . . No matter! I want to break my present
chains and taste life! . . .

[*He muses.*]

Otherwise, I shall have spent my youth in this forsaken
keep—taking on the savage character of the surrounding wilds.
—A wise man as marvelous as Janus will have reared me
more magnificently than kings, vested with a terrible power,
but only a defensive power.—I reign in this frightful Forest.—
Now I feel my heart leap toward countries which are the
gardens of the world with banks reflected by the eastern
seas, toward palaces with marble chambers where
enchanted white princesses fan themselves.—Instead,
like the lord of Hindu tales who does not know
where his treasures are, I should see myself condemned to
languish among these stone walls—tracking beasts of the
woods to calm my despair! No! Even if I must have recourse
to those infernal operations which, at least, remove the
obstacles and pierce the secrets of hell, I will discover that
devastating gold! . . . If I remain a stranger to it any longer
. . . I shall fling myself off a cliff.

MASTER JANUS [*who has read* AXEL'S *mind*]   It was not worth the
trouble for him to be born.

AXEL [*after having glanced at him, as if deciding*]   I know that
according to the ancient doctrine, to gain omnipotence one

124

must conquer all passions, forget all lusts, destroy all traces of humanity,—subdue himself by detaching himself.—Man, if you* cease limiting a thing within yourself, that is, if you cease to desire it; if, by that, you withdraw from it; woman-like, it will come to you, like water filling the cupped palm offered to it. Because you possess the real essence of all things in your pure will, and you are the god whom you can become. —Yes, such is the dogma and first arcana of real knowledge. —Well, that is buying nirvana too dearly: I am a man: I do not want to become a stone statue.

MASTER JANUS   As you wish: but the universe prostrates itself only before statues.

AXEL   What would power mean to me then?

MASTER JANUS   You think so much of yourself?

AXEL [*gloomily*]   Ah! since I have not crossed the dark portals yet, I am beginning to fear a world of ideas—where all my thoughts can roll in vain dementia.

MASTER JANUS   The river fears to become the sea—while losing itself in it.

AXEL   No, the destination is not worth the way to it. What! am I to make the absolute sacrifice only to find in Death, perhaps a dreamless Sleep? a Void? . . . Ah! I doubt—the gods themselves!

MASTER JANUS   The gods are those who never doubt. Escape as they do into the Increate by faith. Fulfill yourself in your astral light! Rise! Reap! Ascend! Become the flower of yourself! You are only what you think: therefore, think yourself eternal. Do not lose the hour doubting the opening door, the moments you inherited in your inception, moments which yet remain for you.—Do you not feel your imperishable being shining beyond doubt, beyond any night!

AXEL   And suppose Death destroys all memory in me?

MASTER JANUS   All memory?—And at this point do you remember yesterday? Is what passes or changes worth remembering? What would you like to remember?

---

* Axel uses " tu " with mankind.

125

AXEL Perhaps my inclinations, resulting from a past of doubts, are a memory. Moreover, who guarantees my persistence as a conscious identity in the supreme ocean of numbers, species, forms ?

MASTER JANUS From this moment on you must acquire the power to become what threatens you in the Beyond :—make yourself an avalanche which is only what it carries along.

AXEL And according to you, what *sure* impulsion would centralize in my being,—even one of those adverse forces ? . . .

MASTER JANUS Spiritualize your body; sublimate yourself.

[*Suddenly with a horrible din, a bolt of lightning breaks one of the vaulted windows, plummets into the room with sparks of fire, a sheet of flame. Darting over the armoury and the objects on the wall, it tears toward the fireplace, furrows it, and disappears.*]

AXEL [*after a pause*] See, Master! how can I take a thought seriously—when this wretched accidental bolt of lightning could interrupt it forever by annihilating my being?

MASTER JANUS [*impassively*] Your *being?* no; your *becoming,* this beggar's pack ! A grain of sand would suffice for that operation. And you hesitate to shake off this dependency, to free yourself ?

[*While speaking,* MASTER JANUS *turns toward the blasted window; he looks into the black and sombre atmosphere.*]

[*It now happens that the air grows bluer, clearer, lighter. The rain stops; the distant noises grow more peaceful. The storm, so it seems, has spent itself in this last thunderbolt. The night is serene; the woods lie beneath a calm enchantment.*]

[AXEL *is astonished by the night, suddenly peaceful. Then he goes back to the fireplace and sits down. He looks at the lamp* MASTER JANUS *has lit.*]

AXEL What strange glimmers that lamp casts ! Is it the old Isaiac lamp the Rosicrucians found in Palestine ?

[*Thoughtfully.*]

Perhaps that flame which looks at me illuminated Solomon.

[*He meditates a few moments.*]

Solomon !—That name awakes a world of dreams in me !—

126

Ah ! who will show me the way to the Ring ! the Ring as it glows somewhere beneath the Orient Sun in the hidden sepulchre of the Prince of Magi !

MASTER JANUS The tomb of Solomon is in the breast of him who can conceive the Light-Increate.

AXEL The Light-Increate, what Everyman simply calls God.

MASTER JANUS If you do not understand the meaning of certain words, you will simply perish in the air surrounding me. Your lungs will not support its stifling weight.—I do not instruct; I awaken.—If you did not have beneath your closed lids a sight already marked by this *Light* which penetrates, recognizes, and reflects the substantial Spirit of things, the spirit of universality among things, when you were puling in your swaddling clothes, I cannot give this sight to you now. If your eyes are alive, if your feet are free, observe and advance. Only you can initiate yourself.

AXEL [*resting on his elbows,—and smiling with melancholy*] And . . . would I then become one of those wakeful magicians, whose genies, darting with torches underground, light up jumbled gems ? Shall I be able to transmute metals like Hermes? displace magnets like Paracelsus? resuscitate the dead like Appollonius of Tyana ? Shall I too find pentacles effective against Fatal Mishaps and Night Terrors ? electuaries to compel or dispel love ? the Magistery of the sun thereby to govern the elements ? the Elixir of long life ? the Powder of projection like Raymond Lulle ? the Philosopher's Stone —like the Cosmopolite? Will I be like the magi of the great tradition ?

MASTER JANUS [*impassively, standing in the pool of blood*] The real " Magi " do *not* leave their names in the memory of passers-by and are forever unknown to them. Their number is the same since time began, but they form a single spirit. The dreamers whom you just mentioned were useful, mortal wise men.—They were not among the Emancipated. The real Magi, if they deign to live, do not deign to die.

AXEL [*trembling*] Then what would a magus be?

MASTER JANUS [*with a vague knowing smile*] If you are anxious to learn the very answer you're seeking—ponder first this simple, discreet question: *How does it happen that even the idea did not occur to you to consider me threatened also by that danger which just passed over us a little while ago?*

AXEL [*surprised, thoughtfully*] That's true! . . .—Would you be? . . .

MASTER JANUS [*curtly*] I am a man who stands before you.—As for these words, exhumed from the old hermetic language, which you take pleasure in reciting, they seduce a youth of your intelligence much more by the brilliance of their sounds than by their meaning. They suggest mere cerebral sensualities to you. You are at an age when the scintillation of the stars constantly prevents your perception of Heaven.— Instead you should forget expressions which are purely verbal on your lips, for you literally cannot yet hear their quick sense. Do not play with them. Each word of yours hovers over you a few moments, then . . . leaves you.

[*He walks to the broken window, opens it with the gesture of a man who pulls aside a veil, then points to the becalmed air and stars.*]

—Instead look at the skies : Where there are no skies, there are no wings !—Be transfigured in their silent light : plan to grow through meditation, to purge in the fire of trials and sacrifices the infinite influx of your will ! to become an adept in the Science of the strong ! to become at last an intelligence freed from the vows and bonds of the moment, in the sight of sempiternal Law.

AXEL [*with a vague heartfelt discouragement*] Who can know the Law ?

MASTER JANUS What can anyone know that he does not recall ? You think you are learning; you rediscover yourself. The universe is only a pretext for this development of any conscience. The Law is the energy of beings ! it is the living, free, substantial Notion which in the realms of the Seen and the Unseen moves, animates, immobilizes, or transforms the totality of all becoming.—Everything palpitates with it !—Your existing weakens or re-enforces it within you and fulfills you in each pulsation, as the result of each fulfilled choice.—You originate in the Immemorial. Now you are incarnated beneath the veils of organism in a prison of relationships.—Lured by magnets of Desire, the original lure, if you surrender to it, you add further oppressive fetters to your chains. The Sensation that your spirit caresses is going to change your nerves into leaden chains! And all that old Externality, malign, complicated, inflexible—which waits to feed on the quick volition of your essence—instead will sow your precious and sentient grain into temporal reacting substances and contingencies with the decisive hand of Death. Death is the fulfilled choice. It is the Impersonal, it is Becoming finalized.

[*A pause.*]

Does some vague tendency still urge you to seize again the truth of your origin? Espouse within yourself the destruction of Nature. Resist her fatal magnets. Be privation itself! Renounce! Liberate yourself. Be your own victim. Be a holocaust on the loving pyres of August Science—dying ascetically like the phoenix.—Thus, the essential value of your days will reflect the Law; all your moments, imbued with its refraction, will share its perennial essence. Thus, you will annul every limitation within and around yourself! And forgetting forever what was the illusion of yourself, conquering the idea of your being—free at last—you become again in the Intemporal,—a purified spirit, a distinct essence within the Absolute Spirit,—even to being the consort of what you call Deity.

AXEL [*to himself without speaking*] I am a poor king. If the splendour of the paternal treasure were unveiled to me, I could choose freely. But, on the contrary, I have not even sacrifice to my credit! Destiny forces me to live on dreams.

MASTER JANUS [*who has read* AXEL'S *thought*] And what else do you expect to live on?—What do the living live on except mirages,—vile hopes, forever frustrated? Is the one who can choose always free? No, he alone is free who has *opted* forever, that is, who can no longer be tempted and is no longer compelled to hesitate.—Freedom, in truth, is only liberation. If you complain of the absence of danger, you verify the possibility of your enslavement; thus, you invite temptation. If you deign to do this, you arc already succumbing. You have just had a terrestial thought.

AXEL [*abruptly*]   And suppose I should be a man for a moment? Isn't the earth beautiful ? Flaming blood courses through my young veins. The great crime of loving and living ! And you* who believe me lost, remember : everything returns to its natal cause! No matter how I incline the torch, the flame with its natural memory will strain towards Heaven.

MASTER JANUS Each time you " love ", that much more of you dies. Unless you divest yourself with a single blow of all mercy for the lures of clay, your spirit, heavier with each dream fulfilled, will be penetrated by Instinct, will enchain itself in mortal Weight. And once your hour has passed, you are strictly lost, a toy in the Impersonal, disseminated by all the winds of Limitation, your conscience dispersed in your former desires, all vain sparks. So henceforth never project but on the Light-Increate the sum of your acts and thoughts.

AXEL   I desire the moment of oblivion:—I have the right . . .

MASTER JANUS   In eternity will you recall a moment or a century? How do you distinguish one from the other?—You make each moment of your actuality flow permanently in a circle. You will find the moment again orbicular, infinitized in yourself. Your personality is only a debt you must acquit down to the last fibre, down to the last sensation, if you want to win yourself from the immense misery of Becoming.

AXEL   Ah ! the wise man indeed can amuse himself with Wisdom !

MASTER JANUS   The madman alone can dream of fleeing what he loves.

AXEL   At least I have won the right to breathe upon the mountain before continuing higher ! Let me look at what I abandon, at least in farewell.

MASTER JANUS   Would a really lofty mind, that is, one cleaving to the intellectual ethers of his divine assumption, be intelligible

---

* Axel uses " tu ".

to himself if he asks permission to halt or plunge? Within your mind it is essentially too late for these shadows of unreal concepts, enveloped in the limbo of the unconscious, wherein the vitality of the word is denied. He who stops at the threshold and turns around, surveying proudly the steps climbed, enters into his own glance and redescends. And—as a sign of the extent of his fall—he keeps that same pride he had in his ascent, henceforth just a figment of his imagination.

AXEL I can let myself go in the current of my passions without being dragged along by them, like a swimmer in a river.

MASTER JANUS A torrent which none reascends. Do not deceive yourself, tempted heart! Only an Emancipated Being can dally, skimming the surface of the earth, without ceasing for all that to be in Heaven at the same time.—So a ray of sunshine can stray here below and vivify the earth with its beneficent warmth,—without leaving, for all that its natal celestial hearth. Become a creature of light before braving . . .
[*With a slight smile.*]
  our twilights.

AXEL I am enveloped, I say, by the mantle of Apollonius! I have the Lamp—and also the sacred Staff to support my steps on the long journey!—How would so many vigils, studies, so many thoughts, alas! have served me, if I had not acquired the power even to repress . . .

MASTER JANUS In this case your own hope has made you a hypocrite. Upon a sensual body the Mantle frays at the edges, wears thin, gets tattered, letting in gusts from the tombs. In the left hand of the Lewd Man the Lamp flickers and dims, ready to go out. In the right hand of the Wayward Initiate the supporting Staff grows brittle, becoming a branch of dead wood. If on grounds of merit you authorize yourself the experience of unworthy acts without fear of punishment, is that still merit?—If your mind is vested with holy strength and light, cease forever to admit complacently the presence of such thoughts into it.—You infuse with your essence each of your ideas, even such idle ones, and each idea by its very existence becomes one of the virtual moments of the Future

Appearance which your puerile life and death will compel you to make corporeal. For entities vibrate in infinite gestation of what makes them whole until Death puts all in the world of absolutes. Your existence is only the agitation of your essence in the occult uterus where your definitive future—your decisive conception—is elaborated. Thus it is your duty to defeat the world for your own sake.

AXEL Onerous duty!

MASTER JANUS If you wish to lessen it, you pervert it; you check it. Do you expect to make terms with something which has no bourns, to waver uncertain in its conditions without setting a limit to your own anguish? What do you think the disciplinary practices of the ascetic are if not the same steps of emancipation of a spirit freeing and refinding itself, retrieving and enlarging itself in its incommensurable entity! The attraction of any temporal dissipation is only an obstacle—as dangerous as pitiable.

AXEL And—suppose the word of the sons of a woman did not pass beyond ... this illusion of space which covers the earth? —I say no! If this whole menacing doctrine were the great Truth, it would be accursed, for the world would be only a snare eternally set for humanity.

MASTER JANUS Know once and for all that there is no world for you beyond the very concept reflected in the depths of your thoughts.—For you cannot see the world fully, nor recognize it, even to distinguish a single mysterious point in its reality. If, granting the impossible, you could for one moment take on the omnivision of the world, a moment later it would be an illusion again since the universe changes—as you yourself change—at each throb of your veins, so that its Appearance, whatever it might be, is in principle only fictitious, mobile, illusory, impalpable.

And you are a part of it!—Where are your boundaries within it? Where its within you? ... It is you it would call "world" if it were not blind and mute! It behooves you to detach yourself! emancipate yourself! vanquish within yourself the fictions, mobilities, delusions,—the very *character* of your

132

apparent world ! Such is the truth, pursuant to the absolute which you can intuit, because Truth itself is only an indeterminate concept of the species you provisionally inhabit, which lends to Totality the forms of its spirit. If you want to possess the world, create it ! Like everything else ! You will only carry away, you will only be, your creation. For you the world will have no meaning beyond the one you give it. Therefore cast off its veils and confer upon it the sublime meaning of your emancipation ! do not diminish yourself by submitting to a slave's senses so it may clutch and enchain you. Since you cannot escape your own illusion of the world, choose the most divine. Do not lose time trembling or drowsing in incredulous or undefined indolence, or in disputing the changing language of dust and vermin. You are your future creator. You are a God who feigns to forget his quintessence only to achieve its transfiguration. What you call the world is only the result of this feint, and you contain its secret key. Recognize yourself ! Proffer yourself to the Essence ! Child of prisoners, rescue yourself from the jail of the world. Escape from Becoming ! Your " Truth " will be as you conceive it. Is not its essence infinite like you ? Dare then to give birth to the most radiant, that is, *choose* it such . . . because it will already have preceded your thoughts by its being, before *being called* into the form which you can recognise!—Realise at last that it is difficult to become a God again. —And go beyond that realisation: because even that thought, if you stop at this point, becomes inferior : it contains a fruitless hesitation.

This is the Law of Expectation; it is the unique evidence attested by our inner infinity. Therefore, it is your duty to accept the trial, when you are *called* by the god that you bear within ! And here is what those who have dared, who have willed, who in natal confidence have espoused the law of radical material detachment and conformed their life, all their acts, and their most intimate thoughts to the sublimity of this doctrine, emancipating their being in asceticism.—And here is what suddenly these elect of the Spirit feel emanate from themselves or originate from them from all parts into the vastness : thousands and thousands of invisible vibrating threads on which their Will courses upon the events of the world, on the phases of destinies, empires, on the influent light of the stars, on the unleashed forces of the elements ! And, more and more, these threads grow in potency with each degree of purity reconquered! It is the sanction of Expectation. It is the threshold of the occult world.

AXEL [*deeply preoccupied, scarcely listening, as if already unable to believe or understand any more*] Oh! this torrential radiant wealth !—it is not just a treasure any longer ! no : it's a talisman.

MASTER JANUS What puerile words, the daughters of Instinct, terrestrial vapour, have you just uttered? You judge yourself " poor ", you who with a glance can possess the world ! You also want " to buy " like a human being, and draw up contracts, wave papers—to be SURE that you possess something ! Thus, you would not consider yourself the master of a palace you contemplated unless by a treaty you become the prisoner of its stones, the slave of its valets, the envy of its guests who roll empty eyes at you ! When you ought to be able to enter and by your sole presence and sovereign glance have all the vassals come obey you—and then the apparent " master " of that same palace would bow before the light of your countenance and tell them stammering :—" Address yourselves to him ".—Does the malady of Youth disorient you so much that you have forgotten all this ?—Well, if its drunkenness overrules you, then, indeed, it is as salubrious for you to possess ringing gold pieces as to possess visionary maxims. If you want to carry a purse, you must fill it. But here is what you must decide since you have fallen so low that you are able to choose : determine your course. Tell me whether you are still free to banish this vain obsession with the gold from your thoughts ?—You hesitate ? you see, don't you, that you are not free because you are not emancipated.

AXEL The branches of the Tree of Knowledge are cold. Indeed, what are the fruits that their icy flowers produce ?

134

MASTER JANUS Understanding is the reflection of creating.—If
you desire other words . . . Weren't you trying to read a little
while ago ? Resume your reading. Perhaps the book will
answer you better than I.—I offer only what suffices.

AXEL [*approaching the folio which has remained open, reading
aloud*] " Fulfillment is yours if you will it! the vibrant Will
which breaks and transforms the forces of Nature ! the sway
of hidden forces! the succouring possession of Virtue, emancipation from proscribed temptations ! the love of Good for its
pure sublimity; communion with the *Reason for Being*, in
short, Total Dominion over the world of appearance—your
shadow !—vanquished and transformed into YOU again.
" Then, genius, transported by celestial Instinct, you will
trample with your intrepid feet the summits of the empyrean
heights, the sanctuary of the World Spirit. Penetrated by your
Ideal, filtered through it, bathed in astral fires, regenerated
by the trials, you will be the essential contemplator of your
transfiguration. Inaccessible to the calls of Death and Life,
—that is, to what is still *you*—you will have become a conscious, infallible, dominating free force in the realm of
Light ".

[*He muses a moment, then with melancholy.*]
O promises based on the benevolent complicity of chance
happenings,—and which are offered to me in unpersuasive
and presumptuously solemn words ! Who guarantees my last-
ing—my forcing myself towards the World Spirit, my reaching
that state of glory ? If I study myself, reed of a single day,
thrall to the passing hour, what am I? A small part of
humanity . . . and what is Humanity ?

[*He smiles disdainfully.*]
MASTER JANUS It has given you the contemptuous smile which
does violence to its maternal dignity.

AXEL [*growing sombre*] So I am a spirit of refuse, a wisp
of straw, a child ?

MASTER JANUS So rebel. A mountain, too, is a wrathful eruption.
Let's see the height of yours !—Too late, your soul has laden
itself with the mental weight of this gold. You think you are

135

rebelling, and you do no more than obey the lower instincts which are already agitating you, so that your rebellion already is no more than the very form of your punishment.

AXEL Master Janus!

MASTER JANUS Ah! choose. I am waiting.—Your silence alone will suffice me. A single indifferent or wrathful word, and I will leave you forever.

II

The Renunciator

AXEL [*to himself, after a brief pause*] The man who reared me is a stranger now.

[*He sits down and muses.*]

Quick forces which assemble the laws of substance, occult Beings which give birth to generations of elements, accidents, phenomena,—oh! if you were just not impersonal! Suppose the abstract terms, the hollow symbols wherewith we veil your presence were only vain human syllables! And suppose that in the chain of infinite contacts, there were a point where the Spirit of man, released from all mediation, could find its link with your essence and be assimilated by your energy! Why, why should this not be so? What would be an Infinity brutally deprived of this possibility—so probable, so natural?

[*As if lost in thought.*]

In the name of what truth could Man condemn one doctrine if not in the name of another doctrine with principles as open to question as those of the first? And, another age, other principles. Science states but does not explain. She is the eldest daughter of chimera. Thus all chimera have the same basis as the world—the most ancient chimera—*something more than* Nothing . . .

[*Abruptly.*]

Ah! what difference does it make to me! it is too gloomy! I want life! *Not more knowledge!*—The Gold is fated; that is the word from the Earth.—Spheres of holy Election, since you, too, are never more than just *possible,* farewell!

MASTER JANUS It is your task to render real what, without your will, is merely possible.

Do you accept Light, Hope, and Life?

AXEL [*after an extended pause, raising his head*] No.

MASTER JANUS Then be your own apostate.—Bathe your flesh in your spirit. Clothe the nude lines of creature forms with your desires. Disperse yourself! Multiply the links of your chains! Become them! Become your very entrails! Taste the fruits of reprobation and anguish; you will soon spit out their ashes because they are like the fruits growing by the Dead Sea. Enrich by one entity more that world of darkness where extinct wills suffer for not being passionately launched in disdain of all things towards Light-Increate! No more high hopes, redemptive trials, supernatural glory; no more inner tranquility. You have willed it thus. You have become your own judge, and you will bring yourself low. Farewell.

[AXEL *has folded his arms. He remains staring without speaking.* MASTER JANUS *has approached the stone stairway; he signals with his outstretched hand.—In the depths of the night a bell tolls once.*]

SCENE 2

[MASTER JANUS, AXEL, GOTTHOLD.]

GOTTHOLD [*entering*] My Lord, I must inform you that Walter Schwert and the major-domo met a carriage on the road. They had to guide the horses to the castle.—The traveller is a woman in mourning; she asks to be taken in.

AXEL [*distractedly, to himself*] Ah! the woman who asked her way to this fortress the very moment she entered the Forest, and to whom I sent guides . . .

GOTTHOLD She raised her veil a moment in front of the fire in the lower hall.—She is a very beautiful young woman, but I have never seen so pale a face.

AXEL [*turning around*] Well, look!

[*Dumbfounded,* GOTTHOLD *recoils a pace when he sees* AXEL'S *dreadful pallor.*]

Wake one of the young castle maids; have the servants light lamps and make a fire in the least dilapidated bedchamber. Inform the visiting lady that the Count of Auersperg pays his respects.

138

GOTTHOLD It is already taken care of, my Lord, and I precede this unknown lady whom Elisabeth is escorting to the chamber of the chatelaine.

AXEL Very well.—Why don't I hear Ukko?—It should be his . . .

GOTTHOLD [*lowering his voice*] He is in the mortuary with Miklaus, Hartwig, and Herr Zacharias, helping with the shroud. I must join them in a moment. It is best that we alone carry out this task.

AXEL Ah! that's right,—I had forgotten.

[*He turns around, sinks into one of the armchairs and rests his elbows. He looks entirely withdrawn from his surroundings.*]

SCENE 3

[*The same,* SARA.]

[*Further back beyond the threshold of the hall* SARA *appears. She is wearing black with a mourning crape over her face. She is preceded by a young girl in the peasant costume of the Black Forest. The servant holds up a lighted candelabrum.*]

[*In passing from the outside into the vestibule* SARA *crosses the wide-open door. She half turns towards the hall and perceives* AXEL *who does not see her since he is leaning on his elbows toward the fireplace.*]

[*She watches him a moment,—then, continues to cross, and disappears.*]

MASTER JANUS [*to himself, from the top of the stone staircase*] The Veil and the Mantle, both renunciators, have intersected : the Work nears fulfillment.

PART IV
THE PASSIONAL WORLD

I

Trial by Gold and Love

[*The gallery of sepultures beneath the crypts of the fortress of Auersperg.*]

[*The family escutcheon, sculptured into the rear granite wall, dominates the tombs.*]

[*At right and left along the complete length of the hall are mausolea of white marble.—Statues of knights and chatelaines, the former standing or kneeling upon their tombs, the latter, wearing the costumes of their particular century, their hands joined in prayer, are stretched out the length of the sepulchre blocks;— sculptured marble greyhounds at their feet.*]

[*A funerary lamp suspended from the central vault dimly lights the mortuary.—Near a porphyry holy-water fount is a large prie-dieu in ebony with worn cushions of violet Utrecht velvet and tarnished gold tassels.*]

[*At left at some distance in the passageway, in the angle of the wall, there is a high terrace window with panes bearing an iron rose-window tracery on the outside; black drapery half conceals it. Near left centre there is a low door hollowed into the thickness of the wall.*]

[*At right at the back of the gallery and opposite the door above, three steps lead to a massive ogival iron door with two leaves which open onto a steep spiral stone staircase.*]

[*In the centre a bronze perfume-pan on a tripod burns low among the tombs.*]

[*At left near the wall* GOTTHOLD *and* MIKLAUS, *each leaning upon a spade, watch* HERR ZACHARIAS *who uses a silver brush to write on an ebony cross the name of the defunct whom they have just buried.—At right* HARTWIG *arranges various objects on a stone ledge.—*UKKO, *smiling, resting his elbows on the prie-dieu, remains standing and watches* HERR ZACHARIAS *also.*]

[UKKO, GOTTHOLD, HERR ZACHARIAS, HARTWIG, MIKLAUS.]

UKKO The epitaph? here is one:—Here lies a carefree lord who loved good cheer and beautiful women. And add this : may his superlative sword intercede for us now and in the hour of our death!

GOTTHOLD Less racket, noise-maker ! This dead man is entitled to silence.

UKKO I do not give heedlessly the title of *dead* to one who so little merited that of *living*. Here lies a heap of satiations, a glittering wretch, who never loved nor prayed. Hence, appeared, disappeared, laughing or grave, what is he to us ? He mocked everything; everything mocks him. One last shovelful and good-bye !

GOTTHOLD Let's be quiet, Ukko!

MIKLAUS One spectre is like any other after the final hour!

UKKO That thing? I defy even both of you together to try to extract a spectre,—from that pierced and emptied wineskin.

GOTTHOLD Childish anger! rash anger of a stubborn . . .

UKKO [*smiling*] Indignation, present at birth, does not wear out; it grows with life; it cannot be travestied with the name of anger.—Come now; lions and jackals, if they seem to be equals because they are both animals, know through all eternity that they do not have the same nature.

MIKLAUS [*joining his hands on his spade*] My boy, you frighten us.

UKKO You think what *I* dare to say.

GOTTHOLD How quickly *you* judge the dead—you a nursling with milk still on your nose !

UKKO Which of you, if dead, would be anxious to share this grave ? . . .

[*A pause.*]

You see.

MIKLAUS [*thoughtfully*] After all, he was a gentleman of brave blood.

UKKO His blood made him brave, not his heart—and he was a

144

gentleman—the way a well-rubbed copper ducat is a goldpiece. What is a counterfeit coin worth ? Less than its metal.

GOTTHOLD Hush!

UKKO Who can hear us? Once these massive iron doors are closed again, thunder and lightning could strike here without being heard through these thick vaults; the end of the cavern is lost in the mountain.

GOTTHOLD I mean that these slabs cover neighbours with the same name as his.

UKKO [*coldly*] Honouring him is dishonouring them.

HERR ZACHARIAS [*rising, supporting himself on the large black cross*] Child, his existence like yours was paid for by a god's blood. You are in the season of strength; well, that passes quickly— and your voice will no longer rise so harshly against the shades.—Instead, help me plant this cross firmly in the fresh ground.

UKKO [*murmuring*] A cross for him? that's offering a great deal to one who bothered little about it.

GOTTHOLD *and* MIKLAUS [*scandalized, severely*] Ukko! we are going to lose our temper.

UKKO So be it: but I maintain that he would beg *you* to be quiet if he heard you. Enough of this, I must venerate your . . . customs.

[*To himself.*]

—And indeed, a beam of sunshine or starlight can make even a dunghill sparkle—

[*He pushes the cross into the grave.*]

—So, to chance!

HARTWIG [*coming up and throwing powder into the perfume-pan*] Here is incense.

UKKO Oh! there was no hurry.

SCENE 2

[*The same,* AXEL, *in black cloak and travelling clothes, enters by the low door.*]

145

AXEL   It will soon be midnight. Tomorrow at this hour I shall be far away . . . I come to bid you farewell.

HERR ZACHARIAS [*trembling sadly*]   Oh! you are leaving, my dear master ?

GOTTHOLD [*stammering*]   My Lord, we are very old. A few days hence we shall want your hand to close our eyes.

AXEL [*meeting their eyes, after a deep silence*]   Friends,—friends! my old children !—I must. Forgive me.

[*To* UKKO.]

During my absence, you will be in charge—except over these men whom you love and who love you.

UKKO [*disconcerted, stammering*]   What! you are not taking me with you ? You are not taking me with you ?

AXEL [*very low, with a sad smile*]   What about your fiancée, child! and your fatherland !—On this Easter day I must leave at sunrise without seeing you again. If you want to honour me, well, let them strike up at dawn our most beautiful, ancient fanfares. I shall hear them from afar. They will remind me of proud bygone days. Tonight, if you do not feel like sleeping, drink up and sing ! Bury in the bottom of the glass your memories of ancient glory and former swordplay !—Embrace me.

HARTWIG, MIKLAUS, HERR ZACHARIAS, *and* GOTTHOLD   Farewell, Auersperg !

AXEL [*after having clasped them in his arms one after the other.— to* UKKO]   A little while ago in the forest I wakened the master forester, good father Hans Glück. You should know that he will expect you tomorrow at daybreak for your betrothal.

UKKO   O my master!

AXEL [*embracing him*]   My son!

[*He opens his arms.* UKKO *runs to them and kisses him tearfully.*]

You will find on my table a parchment signed Axel. If I return no more, the castle is yours.

UKKO [*sobbing*]   Alas!

AXEL   Give me your hands,—and farewell. Leave me alone now; and here is my last order : in the future let no one come down here.

146

[*The four old men, tears in their eyes, bow.*]

GOTTHOLD [*in a low voice*] It's the last time we shall see him.

MIKLAUS [*wiping his eyes with the back of his hand*] And in *his* glance we found our daily bread !

HERR ZACHARIAS [*to himself, a little wildly*] O consternation! the great treasure, lost, lost! I have lived too many days since this morning.

[*They walk to the low door.* UKKO, *his hand on his forehead, hesitates a moment,—then with an expression of mute desolation, he returns to throw himself at* AXEL'S *feet and kiss his hand.*]

AXEL Farewell!

[*Sobbing, staggering, the page rejoins the four old men and leaves with them. The door is closed again.* AXEL *throws his mantle on the prie-dieu.*]

SCENE 3

[AXEL *alone.*]

AXEL [*looking around*] Ashes, tomorrow I shall be like you.

[*A pause.*]

Here, " farewell " subsides into its own echo, empty.—Studying these dead bones is like looking into a mirror.—What is the use of speaking here ?

[*He sits upon a tomb, and, joining his limp hands, his expression glazed, he succumbs to the course of a mysterious meditation. At length he raises his head.*]

—O sleepers, O Rosy Cross, my forefathers ! If there are words which would disturb your slumber, I shall forget them —since I need not weary your shades with puerile entreaties and since approaching Death makes the object of my revery mere vanity.

[*He looks at the large sculptured escutcheon on the rear wall, spotlighted by the rays from the hanging lamp.*]

But you granite sphinxes with gold faces, upholding, it would seem, the secret of All-Wealth, come forth, dream creatures ! —O shapes from the beyond I conjure you,—by the most

147

frightful prospect, the indifference of Destiny! I order you to break the usual silence of the solitary skull, which adds the final symbol to the blazon of my dying race. Let this Death's Head give me a clue—either a glimmer from its orbits, or some miraculous act, a word,—to the enigma of these shining stones which ornament its bandeau.—Let it reveal to me, in short, the meaning of these sacred words : ALTIUS RESURGERE SPERO GEMMATUS.*

[He has hardly uttered the words of this device when he trembles, listening to rustling footsteps approaching where he cannot see.]

[Raising his head, he seems suddenly to have forgotten his very words.—He stands as if prey to some human distraction coming from this unexpected sound of steps.]

What is *this*? Is it the wind moaning? For a moment I thought I heard . . . yes . . . the staircase is echoing, and someone walks very softly.—Ukko, perhaps ? . . . No ! a little while ago I forbade anyone to return.

[He peers through the leaves of the wide door to the stone staircase; then with a start of surprise.]

A woman !—I was right. It is a woman.—Ah ! undoubtedly the one who came tonight ! What does this mean ? The torchière, which she holds above her head, keeps me from seeing her face. She is coming down to these remote caverns . . . and without hesitation, as if she knew the way !—From time to time something gleams and shines in her hand.—I think it's a dagger. What is the meaning of this ? . . . But in truth her insomnia resembles mine ! Her step is quite assured . . .

[He glances around.]

What mysterious curiosity moves me? She approaches . . . Ah! I want to know !

[He hides in an angle of the walls.]

---

* Bejeweled, I [the heir] hope to rise higher again.

SCENE 4

[AXEL, SARA.]

[SARA, *wearing black garments, her face half-hidden by crape, raises her torch in one hand and clutches a stout dagger in the other. She pushes the two leaves of the iron door. When these roll silently open, she appears standing on the stone steps.*]

[*Taciturn, she observes the hall interior very carefully. Her darting glance plumbs the spaces between tombs. Then she descends the last steps, enters, closes the door behind her, and fastens the bar of the door panels.*]

[*She walks to the door on the right and bolts it also.*]

[*This done, she stands her torchière on a funerary socle, then goes to the massive wall at the end of the mortuary.*]

[*There, having turned around once more toward the rest of the gallery and contemplated the timeless silence of the statues, she broods a few moments, then looks intently at the strange armorial blazon on the wall.*]

[*Next, stepping up on the rise of a slab, she approaches the Escutcheon which she appears to study with a peculiar attention.*]

[*Finally, joining her hands on the hilt of her dagger, she seems to summon all her youthful strength and presses the blade point between the eye sockets of the heraldic Death's Head.*]

SARA: MACTE ANIMO! ULTIMA...*

[*Suddenly the entire mass of the wall section cleaves into a wide, vaulted opening, glides, and sinks gradually underground in front of SARA—revealing dark galleries with spacious vaulted arches, extending into the deepest part of the subterranean caverns.*]

[*Now it happens that from the summit of the bound fissure of the opening—as the latter gapes more and more,—escape first a scintillating torrent of gems, a rustling rain of diamonds and, a moment later, slithering gems of all colours, bathed in lights, a myriad of brilliants with lighted facets, more ponderous diamond necklaces, countless flaming jewels, pearls.—This torrential rustling stream of lights suddenly floods SARA'S shoulders, hair and gar-*

---

* Courage ! . . .

ments. *The precious stones and pearls dart around her on all sides, tinkle on the marble tombs, and rebound in sheaves of dazzling sparks upon the white statues with the crackling of a blazing fire.*]

[*And as this section of the wall has now sunk more than half underground, from both sides of the vast embrasure thundering and ringing cataracts of gold coin flow to the feet of the darkly brooding girl.*]

[*Likewise right behind the jewelry, rolling floods of gold pieces pour tumultuously from the broken casks, staved in by rust and the pressure of their number.*]

[*The first have piled up and surrendered their own treasure in the intersections of the immense cavern; the others, accumulating behind them in disorder, superimpose themselves and stretch out in a hundred massive heaps. Here and there in the distant intervals reflections of her torch let us distinguish in the depths of obscurity some yellowed bands of parchment sealed by a large imprint of red wax.*]

[*The nearest gold dunes, heaped against the wall panel, now out of sight at ground level,—roll in profusion, rustle, hum and scatter frenetically,—making a vermillion inundation—across the sepulchral passages.*]

[*Next, leaning her hand against the shoulder of a very old statue of a knight,* SARA *straightens up in the centre of all this blaze where the double funerary flame of the hanging lamp and the flickering flame of her torch are multiplied in thousands and thousands of refractions.—Then still pale, grave, eyelids lowered, her mourning garb contrasting starkly with this effusion of splendours, she finishes murmuring her family device which this awesome eruption has just interrupted.*]

    . . . PERFULGET SOLA !*

[*Then, stretching out a hand in front of her, she raises a handful of diamonds at random and for a moment seems just to mirror her face and eyes in their radiant shimmer.*]

[*However, a vague presentiment, probably, of a presence in the*

---

* Alone, the last [heiress] blazes forth !

room makes her dart her glance over the statues, and in the shadows she perceives AXEL standing against a sepulchre and watching her silently.]

[With rapid movements she drops the jewelry, tosses the folds of her black silk mantle over her shoulders.—Two fine steel pistols gleam at her waist. Seizing one of them, she rapidly aims, fires, and hurls away her smoking weapon.]

[Wounded, AXEL rushes toward her; but already she aims carefully at him with the other weapon; second shot.]

[Struck again but merely grazed by the bullets furrowing across his chest, AXEL reaches SARA. The girl, a dagger clutched in her fist, waits for him, ready to bound, lithe and deadly, in the rhythm of his spring.]

[Despite SARA'S speed, AXEL by feinting a retreat, has overpowered her strong, puissant wrist.]

[An instant later, irresistible—although surprised by the extraordinary resistance of his female enemy,—the COUNT OF AUERSPERG holds her disarmed, paralyzed and overturned upon her arm in his iron grasp.]

AXEL [wrathful, dagger raised] I mean to see the colour of *your* blood!

[The sight of the girl's sublime face arrests his blow at dagger point.]

SARA [seizing AXEL'S wrist and bending it violently back against herself] Well, look!

[The point of the weapon pricks her shoulder. Only a few drops of blood spurt out because the COUNT OF AUERSPERG was able to restrain the impulsion of SARA'S movement.]

AXEL [to himself, as if stunned, considering her in bewilderment] O beauty of a forest when lightning strikes!

SARA [sombrely] Strike and forget!

AXEL [releasing her from his grasp] I will let you have the more precious part—and your life.

[SARA crosses to stand near the perfume-pan.]

SARA [contemptuously, after a moment of silence] So you would have me for an accomplice?

AXEL Your pretentions make you giddy. Half of such wealth

would be worth as much as the whole.

SARA   This gold is Germany's, if it is anyone's.

AXEL   Germany's! Not at all.

[*Smiling.*]

The world's !

SARA [*disdainfully*]   A subtle distinction, worthy of thieves of the night.

AXEL [*ferociously*]   Don't forget that I let you live.

SARA [*simply*]   Did I ask you to?

AXEL   Be reasonable! there is enough wealth here to buy many souls.

SARA   Not enough to trouble mine.

AXEL   Anyway, who speaks in this case on behalf of outmoded scruples?—Have you not demonstrated your gratitude for hospitality by two attempts on my life? And where were you when I saw you ? beneath these lamps and holding these jewels. Was this also to *restore* them to Germany ?

SARA   No, since I should have done that only by abandoning them.

[*A pause.*]

Margrave, no one is lord here—and I have come here to seize the lost sceptre myself only because the excessive quantity of this gold transfigures its very name.—In any country what passer-by has not the right to assume royal power when some regal die is providentially thrown before his feet ? Upon the condition, of course, that he raise the sceptre and rule, proving that he really is a king. If he notices this metal so much that he wants to apportion it, he creates for himself—as you have already said—uniquely the duty of humble restitution.—Share it ? . . . How can you divide a ray of light ?—Survive it ? . . . Vanquished as I am, how can I keep from attesting by my death that it was truly legitimate for me to attempt this conquest? After all, I conceived this conquest only as a real sovereign who does not heed vulgar justice.

AXEL [*looking intently at her*]   The sceptre is yours,* intact and entire.

---

* Axel begins using " vous ".

SARA [*gravely, after a pause*] So be it. But who are you?

AXEL [*thoughtfully*] What difference does it make!—Farewell.

SARA Oh! . . . Stay.

[*Thoughtfully and bitterly.*]

> Would I, if victorious, have abandoned the treasure? No. Having come to survey your domain on an evening cast by the die of fate, I should have rejoined my equipage and my scouts awaiting me on the outskirts of your* forest.—Later, once the legend had died down, I should have acquired this manor, familiar to me now, by distant emissaries! . . . In my eyes your** generosity could be only undeserved alms, and the shameful memory would unceasingly vilify my future joy and pride . . . No!—It is *my* fate to . . . disappear.

[*To herself.*]

> Within an hour I shall have drunk the sap of this mortal ring, and we shall be delivered from each other.

[*She looks at him.*]

> But you*** are staggering—and from one moment to the next I see you pale. Just then I must have hurt you with these weapons. I am sorry. I wanted only to kill you. One of the two of us must survive.—Wait.

[*She removes her mourning crape and walks to the funerary holy water fount.*]

AXEL A trifle. Your bullets grazed my chest . . . just barely.— Do not bother!

SARA This lace soaked in this icy water . . . Cold water checks the flow of blood.—Apply this,—here!

[*Having picked up the dagger, she comes up to* AXEL *and silently cuts off the steel buttons of his jacket. Then, casting the weapon aside, she impassively applies to the* COUNT OF AUERSPERG'S *chest the voluminous black veil soaked in funerary water.*]

AXEL [*to himself as he looks at her*] Through these windows the stars envelope her in their mysterious beams. By her apparition the earth defies and tempts me.

---

* Sara uses the " vous " form.
** Then the " tu " form.
*** Then " vous ".

[*Aloud, suddenly shivering.*]

Young woman, this great treasure—which we have just scorned as strenuously as once we fancied it—does not deserve anyone's death, not on the grounds people ascribe to it.—There is a more elusive and sombre circumstance which has just this moment condemned you.* While you were speaking, the reflection of your essence entered my soul; you took possession of my heartbeats ... and already I have your shadow on all my thoughts. Now, if I bear within me my own exile, I am anxious to remain alone in it.—I am *he who wills not to love* ... My dreams know another light!—Doomed creature, you were the temptress whose magic presence reawakened their old hopes.—From now on, my senses tell me, knowing you are alive would keep me from living! That is why I crave the sight of your lifeless body . . . And—whether or not you understand—I am going to become your executioner so that I may forget you!

SARA [*as if stunned, to herself while looking at him in stupefaction*]
O extraordinary words!

[*A pause; then almost to herself, in a leaden voice.*]

If it were true that you alone among the sons of women could knowingly resist the God who lays hold of you—even if it meant destroying your own paradise ...**

[*She trembles.*]

AXEL [*snatching up a heavy chain from one of the tombs*]   I swear ... that I shall close your heavenly eyes!

SARA [*smiling*]   Oh! the sublime moment! . . . Well! no! It is too late. You ought to have struck without letting me glimpse your soul in the blazing of your superhuman words!

[*The* COUNT OF AUERSPERG *makes the chains hiss and whirl around him as he advances threateningly.*]

SARA [*eluding the terrible blow with a svelte bound, throws her arms around his neck*]   No. Here are heavier chains—and . . . and this time you are really my prisoner. *Try* to free yourself! Ah! you no longer can; it is impossible.

---

* Now Axel uses "tu".
** Sara likewise.

154

[Her face upturned, her glittering eyes watching him through her eyelashes, she languishes at his neck. Her coiffure coming loose, her hair cascades and envelopes her. She speaks in pure tones, her words barely voiced, her voice very gentle, almost oppressive.— Sometimes she closes her eyes altogether, and her dazzling grave beauty glows beneath the light of the torch, the lamp, and the gems.—Breathless, her nostrils dilating, her arms languid.]

Be indulgent to yourself, little one! Do I want to live for myself! Do not kill me. What good would that do? I am unforgettable.

Do you know what you refuse? All the favours of other women are not worth my cruelties! I am the most inhuman virgin. I think I remember causing the angels' fall. Alas! flowers and children have died from my shadow.

Let me beguile you!—I shall teach you marvelous syllables inebriating as Eastern wines! I can put you to sleep with fatal caresses; I know the secret of infinite pleasures and delectating cries, the secret of voluptuous sensations where every hope expires. Oh! let my white limbs enshroud you, burying your soul like a flower lost beneath the snow. Let me veil you in my hair so you may inhale the attar of roses of all time! . . . Yield. I shall make you pale beneath stinging joy; I shall be merciful when you are under this torture! . . . My kiss for you will be like nectar from heaven. The first breath of spring upon the savannah is less warming than my breath— mine is more penetrating than the fumes from the perfume vases which used to simmer in the seraglios of Cordova, more laden with oblivion than the fragrance of cedar slivers cloven by magicians amongst the groves of the gardens of Baghdad to shame the flowers of paradise. Find again in my eyes the soul of beautiful nights when you walked in the valleys and gazed at the skies. I am that exile you were seeking to stars unknown!—I would give up all treasures to be your eternal treasure. Oh! how could I leave life without bathing your eyes in my tears—your eyes of hope, those proud blue stars! oh! without making you shiver beneath the deep music of my loving voice!—Oh! imagine,—it would be hideous; it would

155

be impossible. To renounce all this exceeds my courage. Say that you surrender, Axel,—Axel! . . . And I shall force you to stammer upon my lips the vows that will make you suffer most,—and all the dreams of your desires will pass into my eyes to intensify your kiss . . .

[*A pause.*]

AXEL [*eyes closed, sotto voce*] Your name, even if it burn my lips, I must say it! . . .

SARA [*very low voice, her head resting on* AXEL'S *shoulder*] Sara.

AXEL [*dropping the chains*] Sara, I am no longer an exile.

SARA [*without raising her head*] So, you let me live?

[AXEL *enlaces her with the arm that had threatened her and leads her to the violet velvet cushions of the ebony prie-dieu.*]

AXEL [*smiling triumphantly with a somewhat boyish emphasis*] Among kings would not only a madman fail to set your midnight tresses ablaze with these astral gems? Yours alone, yours this radiant mass, this splendour which you have resuscitated —Just let me gaze upon your fateful pallor.—I want to sit at your feet and suffer in my turn the malady of mankind.—That is what loving is, I suppose! Isn't that right . . . Sara?

[*She is now seated. Starlight coming through the windowpanes makes her black silk clothing sparkle.*]

SARA O charming youth who despite my immodest speech has divined his sacred sister!—You surpass all my hopes! . . . I want no adornment but your childlike gaze which makes me so beautiful. And it is because so great a love subjugates me that I grow so pale.—As for our great wealth, let us live with our starry dreams!

[*He is now seated on a cushion at* SARA'S *feet.—He has folded his arms on the beautiful girl's knees. He gazes upon her for some time as if plunged into an abyss of inexpressible joy.*]

AXEL Yes, like a statue of Farewell, you had to come to me in mourning, smiling and bejeweled amidst the tombs. Beneath your night-hued hair, you are like an ideal lily, blooming in tenebrae. What quiverings rise at the sight of you! My love? My desires? . . . You are as lost in them as if you were drowning in the Ocean. If you want to flee, you must flee through

156

them. They crush you, penetrate you, O beloved! they swell and die in you . . . only to revive in your beauty!

SARA [*smiling, inhaling* AXEL'S *hair*] You smell like bright autumn leaves, O my huntsman! You have blended your savage essence with every attar of the forest soul . . . Dearest joy . . .

[*Proud, excited, she continues to gaze upon him.*]

AXEL [*as if in the deepest moment of a dream*] Sara, my virginal mistress, my eternal sister, I no longer hear what you say, just your voice alone . . .

[*Rapturously enfolding her in his arms.*]

Oh! the flower of your being, your mouth divine! In one kiss to become . . . oh! the light of this smile,—to drink this zephyr from heaven, your breath! your soul!

SARA [*drawing* AXEL'S *brow to her breast, then gravely placing her lips gently on his*] My soul? here it is, my beloved!

[*They remain lost in ecstasy, motionless and speechless.*]

AXEL [*re-opening his eyes*] You have shivered.—It is probably the chill of these stones.

[*He gently releases himself.*]

Above there are old rooms—where fires burn night and day . . .

SARA [*smiling*] No, only we make me shiver. Wouldn't you rather await our first sunrise here?

AXEL [*in a sudden transport*] O vision wherein I should like to die! But you are beyond my conceptions! Where do you come from? What was your mortal form before . . . us?

SARA [*smiling*] This interests you? Oh! can it be!

[*She smoothes the hair on his forehead.*]

Truly, what you ask I have forgotten. Since becoming virtually an Empress of the Orient, I know nothing but you. I date from one hour ago ; what preceded that hour is no longer.— If I should descend again into the memories of life! do you want that?

AXEL In what loving inflexions your dove's voice gambols! No, —let your memories alone!—don't disappear in vain earthly evidence ; instead, remain forever unknown to me!—What are we, in the past itself? some illusion of our desire.

SARA My dear spouse, here is the wedding ring given to the

157

chatelaines of my line in token and pledge. See what is engraved upon its antique emerald.

[*She raises her right hand slightly. A family ring cut with an armorial design sparkles on one of her fingers.* AXEL *examines the fatidic jewel a moment. Then after studying it, completely serious now, he looks at her.*]

AXEL [*smiling gravely*] Yes, this would lead one to think . . . that it is destiny!

SARA [*in the same manner*] Indeed, and if the illusion pleases you, dream on ; I shall dream it, too.

AXEL [*standing, deeply anxious*] Since, mysteriously, the illusion seems to be striving to fulfil itself through us, let's have faith in it. Then it will let us comprehend what our beings were awaiting.

[*A pause.*]

SARA [*looking around, as if to dispel their thoughts*] I too have a marble family in a manor in northern France. There sleep my father, Yvain de Maupers, noble countryman—as well as my mother, a holy woman called back to Heaven!

[*Holding hands, they walk to a mausoleum. A woman's statue with hands joined in prayer, is stretched out upon a stone, with a grey-hound carved at her feet.*]

—It's your young mother, isn't it?—Yes, you have this noble brow . . . and see, what melancholy! Oh! how often have I not felt her gentle hand pressing invisibly on mine when I opened her Book of Hours at the convent!

[*She bows, then in a low voice.*]

Madam, you see: I give your child all that I am.

AXEL [*raising his head*] In the convent?

SARA [*moving away, her hand resting on* AXEL'S *shoulder*] I am speaking of an abbey where my whole young life was detained . . . I believe I remember that I even suffered there.

AXEL [*trembling—in a low, contracted, clipped voice*] Ah! tomorrow the beggar will sit down on some scattered stone of that pile! It no longer exists.—What is its name!

SARA [*in a gentle voice, as with her toe she carefully pushes some jewelry out of her path along the sanded gallery*] O my brother Axel! It is so hard for offences to touch me that forgiving them gains me no glory whatsoever. Think of it! These hearts are condemned to the torture of not loving me. Must they be punished in addition by such a disaster! And if in some past more remote than life they were so misguided as to have created this torture for themselves, are they not ill-fated enough just to possess such a nature? We must only pity them. —After all, they hate me! You could not augment this chastisement of theirs.

[*Thoughtfully,—while the two seem to have forgotten the great treasure.*]

Certainly, in that cloister I have seen cruel eyes where Faith burned only when reflecting the light of an executioner's torch. To those eyes the sky does not seem dark enough. For them it is fitting that the smoke of the stake blacken the clouds. I have heard the beating of threatening hearts,—in which a distraught Fear of a God— . . . that is, of the idea they have of God!—is so blind that they think it is Love;—hearts in which the " Beginning of Wisdom ", its limitations unheeded, is arrogantly mistaken for Infinite Wisdom.—Do they not hope that retribution befalling their white-garbed fugitive will soon justify the prayers which undoubtedly they are offering this very moment for my safety ?

[*Smiling, then sadly, little by little.*]

So let them pity me or condemn me . . . to keep countenance ! In my formidable mercy I leave them the unworthy thought they have of their liberated novice ! Really, what could these consciences, compounded of inhuman rigour, accuse me of before any God when they could never set obstacles to my hope ? My soul but little fears such wicked judges, who dare thus affront the terrible wrath of the Dove.—Those veiled hearts are innocent like stagnant wells, I am sure ! A well can say too : " I reflect the Light ! " Everything reflects light. Therefore, they have a statement as true as any other, but . . . to each his own infinity !—Forget all this, let their own souls punish them ! *I* deign to punish a well—only by flying over it.

AXEL [*whose voice trembles leadenly*] The name of that abbey!

[SARA *looks at him again.—Only now does she recognise just how inexorably her words have fired the indignation of her young soul's intended. Reprisals of carnage and arson flame in* AXEL'S *eyes.— He will be sure to execute his dreams of extermination during his first days of omnipotence.*]

[*She shudders at having enveloped him in this vast avenging love. After an extended pause, she drops to her knees before her young lover.*]

[*Despite her black garments,* SARA *is completely illuminated by the lamp, the scintillations of the precious stones scattered around her, and the bright flame of the nearby torch. She rests her pale hands upon the heaving chest of the young man.—The latter draws back, seized in dismay, as if stunned.—But she follows on her knees across the sanded mortuary passage.*]

SARA [*in a strange, grave voice*] Axel! forgive that holy prison,—in the name of the stained-glass windows where the evening light was so beautiful to me! in the name of the organ which sobbed so bitterly beneath my fingers! in the name of those cold gardens where my melancholy so often sat! . . .

I intercede also in the name of a very young girl, pale like us, but more like the seraphim of the exile—and whose heart, born consumed by love, was so enrapt with sacrifice . . . that she gave me the flower of her white dreams ; she would lose herself for my sake!

Pity! in the name of that child whom I left disconsolate! Oh! because of her pure eyes, still clouded by the thought of me, alas! surely her God will deliver her from my shadow,—because of her celestial and solitary tenderness—I beg of you!

AXEL [*after a shudder, leadenly*] I forgive that dwelling and its hosts—only in memory of this night when I saw you.

[*He stops, his eyes staring, his fists clenched.*]

SARA [*standing, radiant, embracing him and kissing his forehead*] Axel! my young king!

AXEL [*going with her to the prie-dieu and noticing her sombre, shimmering garments apparently for the first time*] But why this mourning on our night of joy, Sara? . . .

SARA [*with great simplicity*] This is not mourning for a human

160

being.—I have known none who merited this badge of sorrow, —but for a more obscure dear friend—oh! so humble! so lost among things! . . . See,—you who alone can understand me!

[*She draws a faded flower from her bosom.*]

Pretend we are alone on earth, lost between dream and life, and look at this mysterious flower, Axel!

[*Harps in the shadowed background play the chant of the Rosicrucians.*]

—See the unconsolable rose!—She appeared to me in a deserted enclosure on a dawn of danger: I was fleeing! I was leaving the cloister of Saint Apollodora. My white vestments, clutched in haste from the mystic feast, were blending in the snow with heavy flakes falling from the branches of the protective forest trees to efface my tracks. Armed with this stout dagger against our *fellow creatures* and also against the forest beasts and still dazed by the light of the tapers, I listened in the night to the distant bells, pealing once more to earthly echoes the birth of the infant Emmanuel, alas! for whom I was supposed to want to die.—Suddenly, in the light of the last stars this miraculously blooming flower, victorious over Winter like me, attracted my notice, and my vision of it seemed a part of me! Is not the harmony between things and beings infinite? . . . This royal rose, symbol of my destiny, a kindred and divine *correspondence* wasn't I destined to meet it at my first step? Its bright miracle saluted my first morning of freedom! It was like a supernatural guide, *an image perhaps fixed by a single word when I had incarnated myself the preceding hour.* She made me tremble, this flower, which seemed to be begotten of my own soul! Undoubtedly she recognised my lips, Axel, when, scornful of all the peril I was in, I told her my great hopes in one long kiss!—Silent beneath my maternal kiss, she still was begging me to pluck her; I felt that in my heart. Gently then I took her entire sharp-thorned stem from the dead bush supporting her when she burst into bloom. Then, holding her between my hands, I warmed the whisper of her perfume beneath my breath while I still held this hermetic dagger, forged in olden days.

161

[*She points to the cruciform dagger now lying on the ground.*]
   Listen! Spirits,—or perhaps . . . genies were surely enclosed in
her beauty! . . . For immediately passages in human History,
until then veiled in my mind, lit up my memory with august
and supernatural significance. Thus I understood, without
being able to explain even the interest I took in understanding,
why this flower so placed by chance upon the cross of the
dagger between my hands formed the Sign which in former
times had dispersed the proudest and mightiest empires like
sands in the wind. This very Sign, I have *seen* it, just now
sparkle on each of these tombs,
[*She points to the pistols thrown to the ground.*]
   in the fire of these treacherous weapons,—when on you . . .
[*She wraps her arms passionately around* AXEL.]
AXEL You say the flower inspired you, Sara?
SARA Oh! a thousand thoughts! . . . I remembered, for example,
that one of the seers of Humanity had made use of the form
of this flower to express in his poetry the sacred, vermillion
circles of the paradise of New Hope!—Then in spite of the
cold, I could not muse on the mocking pretences of mankind
without smiling—when I recalled that the gravest, oh! the most
industrious of peoples had fought a century-long fratricidal
war over roses.
[*A pause.*]
   Yes, she was my sole companion and my mysterious love down
the long road I walked in pilgrim guise.—I kept my eyes
upon the star which shines over your forests, while the other
passers-by shouted insults in the twilight! And the dear
perfume of this succouring flower revived me until I reached
the first large city and sold my pearl and opal necklace to Jews.
For until then hunger, wakefulness, and sleep exhausted my
lonely feet.
AXEL [*on his knees at her side, kisses her feet*] Oh! let me burn
my lips on your pale feet, the glory of future marbles.
SARA [*her eyes on the dead flower*] At sunrise I used to sense
that it would be sweeter for her to die on my breast than to
be reborn in exile from me. This is why I wear mourning for

her enchantment now that her living attar has escaped from her to the highest essence of her light. Loving me, she wanted to perish in my shadow!—Please, let me brush your dear eyelids with her petals! . . . See! . . . She seems to revive!—she mistakes your young tears for dew!—But instead . . . No, —no! I want to be cruel and pluck her petals over you, my knight, to presage all the abandon my love will invent to ravish you!

[*In silence she plucks the flower over* AXEL'S *brow and hair. Then she suddenly becomes grave.*]

—How happy I am to see that if I speak of it ever so little the phantom of a dying flower interests you . . .

AXEL [*covering her hands with kisses and looking at her delightedly*] I love you.

SARA [*standing near* AXEL *and resting her elbows on the prie-dieu, speaks as if she were following between her half-closed eyelids a sequence of dream mirages*] Tell me, dearly beloved! Do you want to come to those countries where the caravans pass in the shade of the palms of Kachmyr or Mysore? Do you want to come to Bengali bazaars to choose roses, fabrics, and Armenian girls white as ermine pelts? Do you want to raise armies—to stir up northern Iran like a young Cyaxares? —Or instead, suppose we get underway for Ceylon, land of white elephants with vermillion turrets, fiery macaws in the foliage, and sun-dazzled dwellings where fountains cascade in marble courts?—For a few days would you like to live a strange and remote existence in those porcelain habitations of Yeddo around the Japanese lakes? There beneath the moon bloom tufts of barbarous flowers like sheaves of perfumed daggers. In the evening, we might like to return smoking opium in gold and jade pipes to the rocking of palankeens.—Would you rather see me bathe in the waves mirroring great Carthage, near a basalt house where perfumes burn on silver tripods?—Or suppose we visited the red Spains! Oh! it must be sad and marvelous at the palaces of Granada, the Generalife, the rose-laurel groves of the Cadiz of Andalusia, the woods of Pamplona where there are so many lemon trees that the

stars seen through their foliage seem like flowers of gold !
And the ruins of Saracen temples, Art now extinct, the morose
cities !—And, farther on, the Blessed Isles where flowering
winter puts the springtime of other lands to shame ! There
you find rocks which dawn transforms into immense sapphires
and where the tide expires in a mist of gold and opal, gentle
as a final kiss.—If you prefer, we shall realize dreams of
glory, we shall accomplish sublime tasks ! the people of the
earth shall bless us !—But if you wish we can try also going
like nomads upon the roads; clad in tattered finery, you with
a blunderbuss at your shoulder and I with a harp at my waist,
like bronzed Tziganies, we shall sing along the roads and in
the Bohemian city squares. I shall tell fortunes to beautiful
girls, and the silver pieces people throw in our wooden bowl
will buy our evening meal in the inn ! Thus we could make
our way singing from the south of the land of the Bulgars
to the strait of Bab-el-Mandeb.—Do you want our carriage
wheels to grate sparks from the paving of the quays of the
Neva or the Danube? Perhaps you would like to see Polish
and Hungarian women dance gaily to music in back of
palaces ?—Shall we be daring adventurers in a steel cannon-
armed brig and skirt the Archipelagoes exploring from Guinea
to the silent Hudson banks ? And then go up the Nile ? Let's
light up the interiors of the pyramids of Chephram and
Ozymandias where we could double the golden circle ! Could
we not just as well go to the banks of the Ganges to found
some divine religion ourselves ? Come ! we shall work miracles,
we shall raise temples, and I have no doubt that Heaven
itself will obey us.—Suppose we go some day to gather delicious
poisons in Melanesia and to stroll in Sumatra beneath the
macheneel trees ? Do you want to see my face reflected in
rivers flowing near Golconda, Vishapur, or Ophir? Or shall
we travel in Nubia on the banks of the Zaijr, the tenebrous
river where evening falls without twilight ?—Do you want to
go see Seleucia where the holy apostles took to the sea to go
conquer the world ?—Do you want to live among ruins in
Antioch ?—There, beseeching ivy stops the pilgrim on his

way !—But, instead, let us fly away like halcyons toward the horizons, always blue and calm, of Corinth or Palermo or beneath the portico of Silistria !—Come ! our trireme will pass above Atlantis !—Unless, instead, we go study the nocturnal lights on the land of Idumea ?—Then, too, the Septentrion !—What a pleasure to attach our steel skates on the roads of pale Sweden ! or when going to Christiania by the sparkling paths and fiords of the Norwegian mountains ! Couldn't we also try living in a forsaken snow-covered cottage in some northern village ?—Do you want to see the desolate moors of Wales ? the parks of Windsor and the fogs of London? or Rome, the sombre city of splendour?—frivolous Paris illuminated ?—How strange it must seem to wander through the checquered streets of Nuremburg, the patient mid-night city !—Do you want to trouble the stars reflected in the gulf of Naples or in the lagoons of Venice while you trail in the wake of the gondola some marvelous fabric from Smyrna or Bassora ?—When we are happy together in some Helvetian chalet, do you want to see dawn shine on the snows of Mount Rosa ?—Do you prefer the hammocks of the Antilles to the tents of Bessarabia ? or the voluptuousness of sheer space ? Shall we let the reindeer carry us off over the ice or ostriches carry us over the sand, or shall we watch the peaceful drome-daries kneeling around a tent in an oasis of ancient Heptano-midas ?—Shall we bury ourselves in a Latin existence at Pompeii as if the Caesars were still living? Or do that farther on, towards the more sombre Orient? Come. I shall take your arms amidst the stones which used to be the hanging gardens of Ninevah ! and the ruins once Thebes, Sardia, Heliopolis, Ancyra, Sicyon, Eleusis,—and the magi's city, Ecbatana!—Do you prefer a marble tower near the Euphrates or beneath the Solyma sycamore, or on the Horeb heights ?—Do you want to dream the blissful oriental dream ? shall we establish ourselves as trafficking merchants at Samarcand? You will become some distant queen's ambassador and come to pay me a visit at Sheba. As kings full of cares we shall see the evening sun set the Red Sea waters on fire !—But, if it appeals to you, we can just as well be simple lovers and go to some hut in the Floridas and listen to the hummingbirds!—Do you see, since we are all-powerful; since now we are like kings in disguise, what difference does it make whether we prefer one dream or another? And as for the land of our exile, won't any country on earth be our Isle of Thule?

AXEL [*with a grave smile*] Child!—Radiant child!

SCENE 5

[AXEL, SARA, *then the chorus of retainers and the chorus of woodsmen,—finally* UKKO'S *voice.*]

SARA The sea, O my beloved, I want the limitless sea! Let us first go to Italy! to its marble and flame-coloured ruins, to its luminous gulfs! We shall quickly exhaust its bright exile.— O nights of love in the palaces! ... We shall buy the darkest one in Florence;—do you want to? Florence must *be* as beautiful as Palmyra *was*!

[*At this moment distant voices in song—a chorus of untrained voices muffled by thick subterranean walls—reach them nonetheless because of the profound silence of the mortuary excavation.*]

CHORUS OF MILITARY RETAINERS Our master leaves; the glory of our fortress fades,/ Farewell, lusts of gold, love and strife! / We are very old, and soon beyond life,/ We shall be shades.

AXEL My servants stay up tonight.—It is at my behest that they drink and sing. They salute the departure ... of a stranger.

SARA As soon as daybreak strikes these windowpanes, let us fly to the land of Hope!

[*As if oppressed by the idea of future joys, she closes her eyes and rests her hand upon a marble tomb.*]

—O voluptuousness of living!

CHORUS [*muted by the distance*] Farewell black pride in an iron Past: / With us declines its profound light! / Like a setting sun of a winter night,/ Old world, you cannot last.

[*Suddenly outside the sky fades into blue; a ray of dawn pierces*

166

*the drapery fringe of the semi-submerged window.—Re-opening
her eyes,* SARA *perceives the dawn and trembles.*]

SARA [*shouting*] Day! dawn! Axel! . . . —Look! It is the future
rising!

[*She walks to the window and pulls back the drapery. The bluing
tones of morning enter the mortuary.*]

CHORUS [*from the depths of the fortress*] Fear not! for in that
sleep you'll soon join me,/ Future times!—Let's drink since
change affects us all!—/ And we shall hear the Angel's final
trumpet call/ If an awakening there be!

SARA [*joyful, smiling triumphantly after pointing to the immense
treasure and mingled gems*] It's time for us to leave! Let us
wrap our mantles about us.—Over there beneath the violet
foliage the rays make our furs and weapons gleam already.—
The carriage horses stamp in the dew. O my young lover!
how they will carry us away beneath branches perfumed by
the storm! Soon we shall fly into the luminous mist.—Soon
here is a thatched cottage appearing before us to the song
of birds, its moss roof bathed in a thousand pearls.—What
happiness to drink the morning milk together, standing, smiling
at each other in grass strewn with fallen leaves!—And still
we fly! Soon here are people on the road! then a village!
. . . then a city! . . . more cities! then the sun itself! then
the world!

[*An extended pause.*]

AXEL [*in a strange, exceedingly calm voice while watching her
intently*] Sara! I thank you—for letting me see you.

[*Drawing her into his arms.*]

I am happy, O my lily, my wife! my mistress! my virgin! my
life! I am happy that we are here together, full of youth and
hope, imbued with a truly immortal feeling, rulers together,
unknown to all, shimmering in this mysterious gold,—lost in
the depths of this manor during this awesome night.

SARA Out there, everything calls us, Axel, my unique master,
my love! Youth, freedom! Vertigo of our own power! And
—who knows, some great causes to defend . . . all dreams to
fulfill!

[*She walks again to the dawn light and holds up the drapery.*]

II

The Supreme Option

AXEL [*gravely, his mood impenetrable*] What is the point of fulfilling them? . . . they are too beautiful!

SARA [*a little surprised—turns around to look at him*] My beloved, what do you mean?

AXEL [*still calmly and gravely*] Let go the draperies, Sara. I have seen the sun long enough.

SARA [*anxiously to herself, still watching him*] Pale,—and his eyes staring at the ground,—he is musing over some plan.

AXEL [*in a low voice, pensively as if to himself*] No doubt at this very moment some god is jealous of me, I who am able to die.

SARA Axel, Axel, do you forget me already for divine thoughts? . . . Come, here is the earth! here is life!

AXEL [*coldly, plainly measuring his words*] Life? No.—Our existence is already full, and its cup runneth over!—What hourglass could measure the hours of this night! The future? . . . Sara, have faith in my words: we have just exhausted it. What would all those realities be tomorrow in comparison with the mirages we have just lived through? What is the point of being like cowardly humankind, our former brothers, and buying the effigies of dreams with this drachma of gold, —oboli of Styx—which scintillates between our triumphant hands!

The quality of our hope forbids the earth to us now. What can we ask of this wretched star, where our melancholy lingers, but pale reflections of such moments of dream? The Earth, you say? What has this drop of frozen slime ever achieved? Only what in the context of eternity Time must belie. Don't you see, it is the Earth which has become Illusion! Realize this, Sara: in our strange hearts we have destroyed the love of life—and indeed in REALITY we have become our souls! If we accepted life now, we should commit a sacrilege against

169

ourselves. As for living? our servants will do that for us. Satiated for all eternity, let us rise from the table, and in all justice let us leave to ordinary mortals whose ill-fated nature can measure the value of realities only by sensation, the task of picking up the banquet crumbs.—I have thought too much to stoop to act!

SARA [*disturbed, worriedly*] These are superhuman words. How can I dare understand them!—Axel, your brow surely burns; you are feverish ; let my soothing voice make you well!

AXEL [*with sovereign impassiveness*] My brow does not burn ; I do not speak idly—and the only fever we must heal is our existence.—Dear thought, listen! and then you can decide.— Why should we seek to bring back to life one by one the intoxications which we have just experienced in their ideal totalities? And why should we want to limit such august desires of ours to the concessions due any moment of time? In time their very essence, diminished, would inevitably annul itself tomorrow. Do you really want to accept with our *fellow creatures* all the wretchedness which *Tomorrow* holds for us, surfeits, maladies, constant disappointments, old age? Should we have to give birth to beings marked to the ennui of continuing? ... We whose thirst an Ocean would not quench, are we going to consent to satisfy ourselves with a few drops of water because certain madmen with meaningless smiles have pre- tended that such is wisdom, after all? Why should we deign to reply *amen* to such slave litanies?—It would be a fruitless fatigue, Sara! and hardly worthy to follow this miraculous bridal night when, virgins yet, we still possessed each other forever!

SARA [*her voice enthralled*] Ah! this is almost divine! You want to die.

AXEL You see the external world through your soul, so it dazzles you ! But it cannot give us a single hour comparable in intensity of being to a second of those hours we have just lived through. Real, absolute, perfect fulfillment is the inner moment we have just shared together in the funerary splendour of this cavern. The ideal moment, we have experienced it; so

170

it is irrevocable whatever you call it! If we tried to revive it by moulding in its image the traditionally deceptive potter's clay of external appearance, we should risk denaturing it, diminishing its divine mould, annihilating it in the purest part of ourselves. Let us beware of not knowing how to die while there is still time.

Oh! the external world! Let's not be dupes of that old slave, whom real light shows chained at our feet, and who promises us the keys to a palace of enchantment, when what his black hand hides is a fistful of ashes! A little while ago you spoke of Bagdad, Palmyra, where else? Jerusalem. If you knew what a heap of uninhabitable stones, what a sterile burning soil, what lairs of unclean beasts make up in *reality* these poor wretched towns which appear resplendent with associations in the depths of that Orient you carry within! And what weary sadness the very sight of them would bring you! . . . Listen, you have thought them? that is enough; do not look at them. The earth, I tell you, is swollen like a brilliant bubble with misery and deceit and, being the daughter of primaeval chaos, bursts at the least breath of those who come near! Let us get away from her, completely! violently! with a sacred bound! . . . Do you want to? It is not an act of madness. All the gods adored by Humanity have accomplished this before us, for they were sure of a Heaven, the heaven of their essence! . . . And from their example I judge that we have nothing more to do here.

SARA No! it is impossible! . . . It is no longer true!—It is inhuman rather than superhuman! My lover! forgive me! I am afraid! You give me vertigo.—Oh! I shall defend life! Think of it! Are we to die—now? We, young, full of love, masters of sovereign opulence! beautiful and intrepid! blissfully radiating intelligence, nobility, and hope! What! right away? Without seeing the sun one more time—and bidding him farewell? Think of it! It is so terrible! . . . Do you want to—tomorrow? Perhaps tomorrow I will be stronger, since I shall be part of you!

AXEL O my beloved! O Sara! Tomorrow I would be prisoner

171

of your splendid body! Its delights would have fettered the chaste energy impelling me at this instant! But soon, since it is a law of human nature, suppose our transports should die away, suppose some accursed hour would strike when our love, paling, would be consumed by its own flames . . .

Oh! let's not wait for that sad hour.—Isn't our resolution so sublime that we must not give our spirits time to awaken from it!

[*A deep silence.*]

SARA [*thoughtfully*] I tremble.—But perhaps this, too, is pride! . . . Certainly if you insist, I shall obey you! I will follow you into the unknown night.—However, remember the human race!

AXEL The example I give it is well worth those it has given me.

SARA Those who fight for Justice say that—suicide is desertion.

AXEL That is the morality of beggars whose God is just a bread-winner.

SARA Perhaps it would be nobler to think of the common good!

AXEL The universe is self-consuming. This is the price of the common good.

SARA [*a little bewildered*] What! how can you renounce so many pleasures? . . . Leaving this wealth in darkness! isn't this unfair?

AXEL Man carries into death only what he renounces in life. Really—we leave behind only an empty rind. What makes this treasure valuable is in us.

SARA [*more quietly*] We know what we leave, not *what* we are going to find!

AXEL We return, pure and strong, to whatever gives us the vertiginous heroism to affront it.

SARA Can't you hear men's laughter if they ever learned this obscure story, this superhuman madness behind our deaths?

AXEL Let's leave the apostles of Laughter to their error. Every-day life takes care of them, caning them in punishment.

SARA [*pensively, after a pause*] Death!

AXEL [*smiling*] O beloved! I do not propose that you survive me because I am entirely persuaded that in your conscience you no longer care about this miserable snare called " life ".

172

[*He looks around as if seeking out the dagger.*]

SARA [*raising her head, now pale as a wax taper*] No. In my ring
under the emerald I have a dreadful poison ; let's find the most
beautiful chalice in this goldwork . . . and let it be done according to thy will.

AXEL [*enfolding her in his arms and considering her sombrely and
ecstatically*] O flower of the world!

[*After a pause he leaves and walks to the sparkling heaps on the
floor of the subterranean gallery.—While he searches amidst the
jewels and gold objects,* SARA *takes up large diamond necklaces
lying on the tombs and silently adorns herself.*]

SARA [*gently, turning towards the window*] What a beautiful sun!

AXEL [*returning, holding a magnificent gem-encrusted cup in his
hand, looks at* SARA *intently and speaks tenderly*] Shall we
walk on the plain and pluck flowers of spring? What joy to
feel the morning wind in our hair! Come! Our lips will meet
on the same first fruits! . . .

SARA [*who has divined* AXEL'S *melancholy thought*] No. I love
you more than the sight of the sun. Our lips will leave their
prints on the radiant brim of this cup!—Here, I have an engagement ring . . . also!

[*She draws off her family ring, presses the spring of the emerald
and from the gold setting sprinkles some grains of brown powder
on the bottom of* AXEL'S *cup.*]

AXEL The dew still falls ; some of its bright tears will dissolve the
poison in this sacred chalice!

[*He climbs up on a sepulchre near the submerged window ; and
while* SARA *distractedly caresses a marble greyhound,* AXEL, *raising
the gleaming fatal hanap in his right hand, passes his arm outside
through the window bars.*]

Thus heaven will be an accomplice of our suicide!

[*From the depths of the forest, voices raise a morning song;* AXEL
and SARA *listen.*]

CHORUS OF WOODSMEN [*in the distance*] For joy! for joy! / Up in
the high trees whose death gives us bread ! / When mornings
come, beneath the golden leaves,/ Woodsmen, waker of the
birds, hearken ! / Wind, voices, leaves, wings ! / In the depths
of the woods everything sings: /Glory be to God!

SARA Do you hear them? God? they say!—Even they the assassins of the forest!

AXEL Let a beautiful syllable fall in peace on the soul of the last woods!

SARA [*thoughtfully as if to herself*] I held the axe, too! but—I did not strike.

[*On the plain, reveille and fanfare.*]

UKKO [*in the distance*] On the slope of the flowering mountain./ Here is the bride-to-be!/ Dew on the hem of her white bridal gown,/Traces a pearl design./Let all bow before the bridal maids,/With their innocent German eyes!/And thus her earthly steps will ring.

AXEL Those children are getting married! Sara, utter a word of happiness for them. Some thought of yours will surely make them even more adoring!

SARA [*smiling, turning toward the window*] O you carefree mortals who sing upon the hillside ... blessings on you!

AXEL [*climbing down to her*] The gleams of this nuptial lamp pale before the light of day! It is going to flicker out . . . like us.

[*He raises his cup.*]

Old earth, I will not build the palaces of my dreams on your thankless soil. I will not carry a torch. I will not strike enemies.

May the human race, disillusioned with its vain chimeras, vain despairs, all the deceptions which dazzle eyes made for flickering out—consent no longer to play a role in this dreary enigma, —yes, may the human race end like us, unawed fugitives, without addressing you—old earth—even a farewell.

SARA [*sparkling with diamonds, resting her head on AXEL'S shoulder, seemingly lost in mysterious rapture*] Now, since infinity alone is no deception, let us steal away, oblivious of other human words, into our own Infinity!

[AXEL *bears the fatal cup to his lips—drinks,—shudders and staggers.* SARA *takes the cup, finishes the rest of the poison,—then closes her eyes.—*AXEL *falls;* SARA, *bowed over him, shivers. And*

174

now they lie in each other's arms on the sands of the funerary gallery—their lips exchanging the supreme sigh.]

[*Thus they lie immobile, lifeless.*]

[*Now the sun tints the marbles and statues. The sputtering flames of the lamp and torchière turn to smoke lit by the rays which flood the room obliquely from the terrace window.—A gold piece falls, rolls, and rings like a clock striking, against a sepulchre.—And— disturbing the silence of the awesome place where two human beings have just freely dedicated their souls to the exile of Heaven —are distant murmurs of the wind in the forest vastness, vibrations of the awakening of space, the surge of the plain, the hum of life.*]

FINIS

THE SOHO BOOK COMPANY

THE DEAD SEAGULL, by GEORGE BARKER

I warn you that as you lie in your bed and feel the determination of your lover slipping its blade between your ribs, this is the real consummation. "Kill me, Kill me," you murmur. But it always surprises you when you die.

ISBN 0948166 00 2 / £4.95

THE ENCHANTED WANDERER, by NICOLAI LYESKOV

He deserves the privilege of standing with Tolstoy. (M. Gorky)

ISBN 0948166 04 5 / £5.95

SELECTED LETTERS of FRIEDRICH NIETZSCHE

Visions have appeared on my horizon the like of which I have never seen.

ISBN 0948166 01 0 / £6.95

MARIUS THE EPICUREAN, by WALTER PATER

The only great prose in modern English. (W.B. Yeats)

ISBN 0948166 02 9 / £7.95

ARMANCE, by STENDHAL

A neglected masterpiece. (A. Gide)

ISBN 0948166 03 7 / £5.95

DOMINIQUE, by EUGENE FROMENTIN

I feel myself a child before a man who has reflected so much. (George Sand)

ISBN 0948166 06 1 / £4.95

AXEL, by VILLIERS de l'ISLE-ADAM

Admirable, but mad. (J.P. Sartre)

ISBN 0948166 053 / £4.95

1 BREWER STREET LONDON W1R 3FN TELEPHONE 01–439 0100